Mary Elizabeth Blake

On the Wing

Rambling Notes of a Trip to the Pacific

Mary Elizabeth Blake

On the Wing
Rambling Notes of a Trip to the Pacific

ISBN/EAN: 9783337141110

Printed in Europe, USA, Canada, Australia, Japan

Cover: Foto ©Andreas Hilbeck / pixelio.de

More available books at **www.hansebooks.com**

ON THE WING.

RAMBLING NOTES

OF A

TRIP TO THE PACIFIC.

BY

MARY E. BLAKE,

[M. E. B.]

Author of "Poems," "Rambling Talks," etc., etc.

BOSTON:

LEE AND SHEPARD, PUBLISHERS.

1883.

INTRODUCTION.

A DEMAND from many quarters, — which a servant of the public has no right to disregard, — and the interest evinced by a wide circle of readers, when the letters which make up the larger part of these pages appeared last year in the *Boston Journal,* have induced me to offer them again, revised and enlarged, in this more permanent form. Partly because I think no book should ever be published which requires apology for its contents, and partly because the title of the little volume sufficiently explains its want of elaboration, I shall make no excuse for the casual nature of the following chapters. For what could be expected of one on the wing, but bird's-eye views?

M. E. B.

BOSTON, January, 1883.

CONTENTS.

ON THE WING.

CHAPTER I.

THE first night in a Wagner "sleeper," *en route* for California, is apt to be one of the experiences of life. You have not yet got your sea-legs on, so to speak; you have n't fully mastered the seaman-like roll which is to carry you safely over the heaving deck of the palace car; the management of your equilibrium bothers, and you are just sufficiently dazed and tired to be a little miserable whether or no. When the time comes to enter your bunk, even if it has a double berth, you lose heart still more. It looks so straight, and the curtains so heavy, you bump your poor head getting in and your poor back getting out; you are tingling yet with a sort of sub-acute excitement at the danger and daring of your rash act in going west on a flying trip through the dark, and the spasms of home-sickness, which have been coming and going at intervals all day, begin to settle into a sober ache of longing. In this strait, such minor shocks to your sensitiveness as a glimpse now and again of a gentlemanly young fellow in his shirt-sleeves, or a lady-like young person in her corset cover, become rather exhilarating than otherwise, as proclaiming your release from conventionalities, and as rubbing off that dust of conservatism which naturally

1

clings about any bit of New England society. You peep out occasionally to see how the rest are getting on, until nothing is left but the empty, narrow aisle in the middle, and then at last compose your own decorous nightcap to sleep. But a sense of responsibility remains with you. Every time through the long night that the car gives a lurch, you sit up to ponder its meaning; every time the whistle sounds you draw your curtain to know what it means. A vague impression that the engineer needs watching and guidance rests with you, and weights even your short dreams with personal care. You are not a bit nervous — just as cool as the very hot atmosphere of the car will allow one to be — but you prefer getting up every half-hour to see that things are properly attended to. Farther up, an easy old traveller sleeps soundly and loudly; could habit ever make *you* so selfish?

Your sleepless disinterestedness pays in the end; you get so much more for your money. Why, here last night, in different glimpses, were first an illuminated city — its flaring lights streaming high into the misty air like an Aurora; then a gaunt row of spectral poplars standing like soldierly ghosts in the white moonlight; now a thunderous passage of some flashing meteoric train, and again the shadow of a quiet town asleep on a hillside; once we tore through a tunnel with dismal and awful shriek into the colored signals and electric brilliancy of a great crossing; and once, just as the sky began to change to the faint opalescence of dawn, there was Cassiopeia, low down in the north, with each of her five stars aflame like a

burning torch, looking in at us in a wholly royal manner. And all this thrown in like a side-show at a
circus while you are taking flying leaps through the
darkness at the rate of forty miles an hour! A sym-
pathising friend who heard all this next morning, con-
soled me by the prediction that I would sleep like a
top to-morrow. But people who desire to sleep like
tops should always stay to hum — that is not what we
paid our money and came West for.

"How did I get in a Wagner sleeping car?" Well,
that's neither here nor there. If a busy home-body
chooses to pack her trunk one day and go on a Raymond excursion the next, whose business is it? Isn't
it the only way for a busy home-body to go? If she
stops to consider all the *pros* and *cons*, — the baby's
new tooth, the spring house-cleaning, the chances of
coughs and colds, the children's changes for summer,
the general depravity of inanimate things, in fact,
which works such infernal revolutions in a household
when its natural head is absent, — if she waits to think
of these, — the stay-at-home weight will be so overwhelming in proportion that she could not be pro-
pelled away by anything short of a catapult. She
who hesitates is lost. The only part for a valiant
woman is to buy her ticket, close her eyes, and at one
fell swoop leave all behind her. It was the plunge of
Curtius which saved Rome.

We started on a gray day, teary and dreary like our
feelings, but with occasional bright gleams and fair
promise of a joyous to-morrow. A railroad car is
never particularly cheery, and is too business-like to

be picturesque; but by the time you get your wraps
disposed in graceful negligence, your extra bundles
put away, and the flowers which loving hands have
brought to breathe their sweet message of fragrant
remembrance disposed to the best advantage, your
particular section manages to put on a home look.
You find, too, that of all other places it is the best for
fraternizing. Strangers in the morning are acquaintances at night and friends by breakfast time.

There is nothing like travel for giving a person
broad views of men and things, and crushing in the
bud puerile enthusiasms. For what other reason can
the man who goes to Europe for two months sit calmly
down on his neighbors for the term of his natural life?
For what other reason could we, who ordinarily would
rave so loudly and long over the Berkshire Hills, look
at them now with the supercilious, well-bred indifference of people on their way to Pike's Peak and the
Rocky Mountains? A woman who has a proper regard
for her nervous centres cannot afford to begin to gush
a hundred miles from the start, when she has nine
thousand miles of a journey still before her. The
climax would be too terrific. So we crossed the State
line into New York in heroic silence.

But when we began next morning to pass through
the beautiful meadows of Pennsylvania and Ohio,
when the lagging sun came out at noon and found us
still passing fields as level and green as the baize of a
billiard table, when night fell while we were seemingly
in the midst of that beautiful, fertile, stoneless reach,
we began to talk in spite of ourselves. Fresh from

the rock-ribbed soil of New England, where only by mistake a little earth is occasionally found sifted over the granite foundation, these smooth, flawless stretches of country are beyond any conception we can form of them. Even the rich brown soil, covered now with the faint green of freshly-springing wheat and grain, was not so novel to our eyes as this wonderful free-dom from any vestige of stoniness. The brakeman who heard us commenting so delightedly over this was evidently nonplussed. " I shed be more s'prised ef et *wuz* rocky," said he; "in these parts ef a man scoops in a stun that weighs fifty pounds he hauls it hum an sets it up in his front yard for folks to look at." Towards noon we passed the tragic bridge of Ashtabula, looking calm and innocent enough, span-ning the shallow, brawling stream that danced in the sunshine below it. A little later on, the red roofs of the pleasant farm-house, which its dying master so longed to see, showed themselves beyond the little station at Mentor. There was a group of peach trees in full bloom, shining like a pink flush between the tender green of budding apple trees; the happy fields were smiling at the waking touch of growth, but our hearts went out more in accordance with the sorrow-ing woman who sat by her solitary fireside, than with the living springtime.

As we enter Cleveland I find a disappointment in store. In common with most sensible people, certain words have always had a strange power of exciting me to romance and conjecture. Vinelands and vine-yards belonged to this catalogue; so when they told us we would reach the grape country soon, visions of sunny, sloping hillsides, with shadows filtering through broad leaves and graceful tendrils climbing over rustic arches were in my mind.   It was no use for common sense to say it was not yet summer; common sense is the slave of imagination, and as such ordered about without mercy.   Imagine then the shock, of acre after acre of short stakes, thick and clumsy, as if some enterprising Natick boot manufacturer had planted shoe-pegs for seed and they had grown up, for that was all we saw of the vineyards.   The vines were not yet out of bed; but the city itself is a pleasant one, and shows its kindly side to strangers in the beautiful park which skirts the railroad.

Lake Erie was in one of her surly moods after a long storm, which had riled her naturally placid complexion into muddiness.   There was none of the lovely blue of my beloved old ocean, and even the passing sails of far-away ships could not make it have the proper effect.   We began after dinner to come across little log cabins here and there, and girls and women dowered with that enormous sunbonnet which seems to be a birthright of the Southern and Western pretty maid.   Two rosy-cheeked poppets on the platform of a country station we passed, flirting with an awkward young Hoosier, showed that this sort of inelegant headgear can be made as eloquent as a Gainsborough hat, when the head it covers is young and beautiful.

Still the same level, smiling fields, the rushing train flying in a straight arrow line through them.   There is very little unpleasant motion.   Some drowsy ones are dreaming away on improvised pillows; some are reading; some visiting neighbors; — it seems as if we were already so used to the novelty that we have been here a month instead of a day. At Toledo a sonorous gong, which I suppose is the sort of guitar the Toledo blades use in serenading, woos us to supper. The small boy who bangs it evidently means to earn his money. We find the usual unusually good meal waiting. On this point the excursionists have made a ten-strike; they live on the fat of whatever land in which they happen to tarry.

It seemed, at first, as if a different atmosphere should mark our passage across each state line, — some change of feeling or temperature to mark our progression between the somewhat finical straightness of Eastern limitations, and the broad unfinished mental processes of the West. But though we have tumbled over six boundaries already, I would never have known we had left New England, except for the level country and the queer, slovenly, zigzag fences. And yet the simple consciousness of distance shadows our jubilant spirits as the second day begins to darken, and the thought of home leaves us, like Huldy, —

"All kind o' smily round the lips
An' teary round the lashes."

The porter of our sleeping-car must have moral designs in keeping us so hot. He either wants to frighten us into a belief in eternal punishment, or to frighten us out of it. At five o'clock this morning, when we awoke in the Chicago depot, it would have done

for a page of Dante's Inferno.   I finished my toilet in
the open outer air, rather than smother within.   But
we gave the young African his tip all the same, for
he did it out of kindness.

After one day of walking and riding around Chicago,
our impressions are like a kaleidoscope.   So flat a
place was never before known; it seems as if a spirit-
level had been taken, and even the usual slight curve
of the earth's surface smoothed off.   Then they set
out Chicago.   But they have large hearts and noble
ideas, these Western people.   The stately, broad
avenues go in such magnificently broad lines, straight
as an arrow's flight, from lake to prairie.   The beautiful mansions, each set in its square of green lawn,
give a beauty and oddity to the richer part that the
business portion does not carry out.   Looking from
the Sherman House, one might really be looking up
State street, except for the extra dinginess which the
soft coal adds to the great buildings.   You can almost
feel the smutchiness.   Looking down across the business portions, the heavy smoke clouds hang like a pall
low down even into the streets.   I am afraid it would
spoil a good deal of the pleasure of life here for me.
We have seen wonders and wonders, but who wants
to be bored with details of sight-seeing when they can
come some other time and see for themselves — when
they can roll magnificently through the gas-lit bowels
of the earth with ships sailing above their heads,
or stand in awe and admiration before those four
gigantic engines at the water-works of which one
alone pumps 36,000,000 gallons a day, or see the enor-

mous stock-yards, or investigate the still more enormous grain-elevators. The place is meant for a race
of giants — and they are giants in energy and large-
heartedness. This is why when one of them grasps
your hand with that firm, Western clasp, you feel
no longer a stranger in a strange city, but a friend
made at home by loving kindness, with a strong
support behind you which will back you for all it is
worth.

We are still in the same world as at home, however.
The troops of pretty girls you left in Washington
street are here walking up Clark street with the same
fluffy hair, big hats, and long satin overcoats. Spring
dresses are not out yet, though we were passing
dandelions and buttercups on the fields for hours
yesterday. Men and women may have a shade of
better color in their faces, but otherwise there is no
change. They talk of "blocks" in describing distances
just as they do in New York, and advertise houses
"for rent" instead of to let. They speak with a little
more breadth in their vowels and honest attention to
consonants, wisely thinking that if they were not intended for use the words would have been spelled
without them; otherwise they are bone of our bone
and flesh of our flesh.

The streets on Saturday night are simply swarming.
I think nobody can be left at home, and the wooden
pavements are in the most awful condition, once you
get out of the really busy portion. A ship in a storm
is nothing to the tossing our barouche and poor
bones got yesterday. It is another of the evils of the

republics that such persons as whoever the man may be who took the contract for this work and made such a wretched bungle of it cannot be instantly beheaded, as a salutary warning to his kind.   Two or three summary executions would save enough profanity to work a larger revival than Moody and Sankey's.

CHAPTER II.

THE more one sees of Chicago, the more the difference between it and an Eastern city impresses itself. To walk the streets on Sunday and see furniture wagons moving loads of goods, the doors of hundreds of shops open, while buying and selling went on, and crowds bent on evidently temporal business, mingling with decorous church-goers, was strange enough. But to travel at night, under the glare of gas and electric lights, to see theatre doors swarming with pleasure seekers, brilliantly illuminated stores, immense number of Germans with their deep-mouthed gutturals, and the open halls and pleasure gardens, made stronger inroad still on the hereditary prejudices of descendants of the Pilgrims. If another conflagration had swept the place, like Sodom, from the face of the earth, it would have been to many minds among us only the just reward of its iniquities. Yet what right have we to raise our own standard of morals and make every one else doff his hat in passing? The foundations of religious belief ought to lie too deep for such passing winds to shake; and it would take much stronger proof to convince me that there are not as many saints in Chicago as in Boston.

We found a mild flavor of the great fire still in the air; it will take a new generation to heal the scar. Events reckon from before or after, relics linger in private and public places, and the harrowing memories of ruin and desolation still rankle in many hearts. But this is *sub rosa;* outwardly, the brave, lusty city might be a hundred years old for any trace of ruin or immaturity about it. The same magnificence of resource which shows itself in its 350 acres of stock-yards, in its forest of elevators, in its miles of new avenues, in the stupendous rush of its business streets, is behind everything. It opens the hands and hearts of its people to a hospitality as broad as its dimensions; it puts a fine, impulsive swing into their everyday gait; it makes a background of reality for the fabulous stories of wealth and enterprise which are in the air. You can fully believe that any Chicagoan, as well as the man pointed out, might have found himself, on retiring from business, with a million and a half more than he counted on, or that any other might have answered a friendly sympathizer, with the lordly indifference of Mr. ———— , who indorsed a note for two millions and had to pay it: "O, I never look back at that sort of thing!" You can fully believe anything of a place where porter-house steak costs only sixteen cents a pound; where strawberries come in March and go in November; where the horse cars run without horses; where the people have an amount of spiritual elasticity which enables them to go to church Sunday morning and to opera Sunday night without destroying their usual poise, and where the world is so flat that it seems

as if Dame Nature had mistaken the crust of the earth
for pastry and rolled it with a rolling-pin.

Remembering the markets of Philadelphia and
Washington, we were somewhat disappointed in those
of Chicago. There was nothing distinctive about
them, as compared with the luscious piles of fruits
and flowers, the sweet-smelling heaps of freshly-
grated cocoanut, the tempting pats of butter hidden
under green leaves, and the shining white eyes and
black faces of the turbaned huxters in the spacious
southern quarters. Before you begin to question, you
might be among any collection of provision dealers,
ruddy-cheeked and white-aproned, of your native city,
but as soon as you hear the price list, you know that
this is another world. One does n't wonder that
prudent housekeepers here hesitate about coming to
Boston to live.

We need to come West to understand the luxury
of modern travel. The spirit of enterprise is so ram-
pant here — the population are so constantly moving,
prospecting, investigating, colonizing, that they lavish
time and skill in eliminating every drawback from
the comfort of railway life. As a natural consequence
their cars are the best in the world. The Pullman is
brighter, roomier, and more convenient than the Wagner. The sections are larger; the mattress and pillows
wider and softer; the toilet arrangements more plentiful. Add to this that you have acquired a certain
savoir faire — you know what you want and how to
get it; you have learned to go from one end to
the other of the train while at full speed without too

many false steps. You begin to have a certain home
feeling in the tidy compartment, which is your especial property, with its mirror between the two broad
windows, its portable table and its silver hooks. The
brightest of mulatto boys waits your beck to bring
a clean, white pillow for your tired head, to brush
your dusty clothes, to fetch messages, to gather up
any incidental rubbish of orange-peel or peanut shell or
paper scrap. You can write if the mood takes you, or
play games, or read your neighbor's books; if you
want anything under the sun, from a cambric needle
to a French bonbon, from a postage stamp to an en-
cyclopædia, there are a score of valises besides your
own to choose from. There are books, magazines,
newspapers, maps, guide-books, and time-tables in bewildering array to consult; there are country depots to
raid upon, and country people to startle, at queer far-
away places; there are Mayflowers to gather and
strange beetles to impale at prairie watering stations;
and there are the observations to make that belong to
this new order of things. Each car in the long train
has its own special recommendation; one has the
prettiest young girl, one the brightest company, one
the most elaborate finish, and so on. We modestly
plume ourselves on the most picturesque young man
with the most artistic leaning toward the fine arts, and
the nattiest and laziest little porter of the party,
"which namin' no names, no offence can be took."

Owing to these and a thousand other causes, the
third and fourth days of railroad travel are less weary
than the first. There is always something unexpected

to keep one awake and interested ; a long tract of overflowed country, with pale green cottonwoods growing
out of the water in a ravishing bit of æsthetic coloring, a forest of delicately-tinted trees, a bank of brilliant purple flowers extending for miles along the
track, or the long majestic sweep of some great river,
turbid and furious, with a flight of wild duck winging
their slow way northward. On the Mississippi we
passed a great steamboat — the steamboat of Kit, and
the Octoroon, and Uncle Tom's Cabin — top-heavy to
our sea-used eyes, with a raft of acres of logs floating after it from the upper country. At Joliet we came
upon a crop of rocks for the first time after hundreds
of miles of smooth prairie ; and quarries of stone of
the strangest formation, as if the strata were laid in
masonry. Farther on was a region of coal mines ; at
the mouth of one a miner had just emerged from
underground. He was a solitary and most desolate
figure ; his flannel shirt open from throat to waist, his
heavy eyes lustreless, his face and bare arms as black
as the coal-bed from which he had just risen. As the
train slowly drew up at the tank near by, he stood
motionless, his tired arms crossed over his patient
breast, seemingly beyond being moved to anything
else than weary endurance. It gave me a pang to see
his pathetic figure merge again into the flat landscape.
What right had one part of the world to be butterflies
and the rest grubs ?

But to return to our Pullmans. There was a delicious siesta at early morning when one first woke.
The uncertainty which made the night jerkily anxious

was over; you no longer felt obliged to know what
every twist or jar meant; your faith in human nature
and the employés of the railroad returned, and there
were two good hours during which, luxuriantly indolent, you could doze and dream, or lazily watch the
panoramic world whizzing by your window. The
soothing motion, the novelty, the comfort were indescribable; you could meditate, admire, enjoy by turns.
Your horizon was absolutely free from care. When
it pleased you to get up, you knew that there was
a deft man-of-all-work to change your bed-chamber
into a drawing-room; your breakfast would be ready
at some clean country station, ordered beforehand
by your advance courier; every petty hindrance of
looking after or caring for baggage or checks would
be lifted from your shoulders, and there was no drawback to the blissful ease of perfect freedom. It
would be ruinous if this lasted too long; so you
rather welcome the sudden jerk that bumps your head
against the marble basin while performing your ablu-
tions, and then tumbles you into an opposite corner —
you feel that it makes you square with fate. To be
too happy might anger the gods.

It was lying this way one morning, looking, as I
thought, toward the west, for the sun had set on that
side the evening before, that I saw a glorious sight.
Little by little, up through the night, came a tint of
loveliest amber climbing above the horizon. Little
by little it changed, deepening into mellow orange,
and creeping high and higher, while flushes of rose-
color ran through it, until at last the entire sky was

one burning glory of crimson. While I lay breathless, looking in wonder at such a blaze of reflected light, the great round sun lifted itself above the world, and I realized only then that our direction had changed during the darkness, so that I had really seen day dawn over the plains of Kansas.

It was about this time we were introduced to the altogether delightful idea of the dining-car. Clean, bright, and airy, with snowy linen — the whitest we had seen since leaving home — with tiny sideboards, set above the tables, gay with glasses and a bit or two of Kiota, with a cuisine that would tempt a gourmet, what a nice bit of variety show it made for us. From the speck of a kitchen at one end, about three feet by six, surrounded by ovens, steamers and stew-pans, came a bill of fare with everything from green-turtle soup to canvas-back duck, English snipe, and olives. The cook was a cordon bleu, a real chef in his honorable profession. How he created the forty-seven dishes on his bill of fare from such a mite of a laboratory would puzzle any one but such a black conjurer as himself. I wouldn't mind putting a girdle round the earth at any time with such a commissariat in front of me.

Kansas City is an absurd jumble of ups and downs. We thought at first the inhabitants must be æronauts, who went in balloons to reach their dwelling houses, but on nearer inspection we found goat-paths leading up the edges of the precipices, and graded roads reaching around them by wide curves. Looking at it from the standpoint of babies, it would be a

dreadful town to live in.   A single misstep would roll
any well regulated child from fifty to three hundred
feet, according to locality.   I wonder all the grown-up
people are not cripples.   The business town is on the
flats by the river.   It is a place of great activity.
Thirteen railroad lines begin or terminate in it, and
the result is stupendous.   That train on your right
will take you to Mexico; this on your left to Boston;
just across there is one placarded "For Colorado,
Utah, Idaho, Nebraska, Montana, Oregon and California," which is a sort of multum in parvo only possible in a western station.

Kansas itself is a delightful country.   All day we
rode between luxuriant fields of winter wheat or
springing corn, interspersed with huge stock-raising
farms, each divided by hedges of osage-orange in the
full green strength of early summer.   We saw, too,
substantial walls of stone — a pretty, cream-colored
stone, that makes a charming contrast with the vegetation — and neat, New England rail fences.   The
slovenly Virginia fence, which is neither strong nor
lovely, seems to be discarded.   In these immense
fields, all kinds of mechanical implements, moved by
horse-power, enable one man to do the work of a
dozen.   Such is the luxuriant richness of the loam
that it is absolutely black and seems of inexhaustible
fertility.   It could be a granary for the world.   In the
towns one is constantly surprised by the beauty of the
public buildings, the finest of which is usually the
school-house.   Miles and miles away from any vestige
of civilization, beyond this always beautiful cultiva-

tion, you come upon a commodious two-story farm-house, with a colony of smaller habitations clustered near. Across the prairie roads you seldom see a single horse driven, except for riding; usually a pair of fine animals are harnessed to even the smallest vehicle. Here and there, by the bank of a river, or on some overhanging cliff, the strange geological foun-dation of the country shows itself; a geometrically regular layer of cream-colored stone, two or three feet in depth, set in a deep bed of clay which the touch of time has dried into a resemblance of sandstone. In the distance now and again a beautiful rolling country fills the horizon, or a fine forest of straight young trees comes down to the foreground. Sometimes for miles we follow the course of the river, but ever and always the great marvel to us is the richness of the soil. It is a country of which one might truly say, "Tickle it with a hoe and it laughs into a harvest." I can see the old New England farmer who sits opposite growing gray hour by hour as he looks upon this para-dise of produce lands, and thinks of the rocky hill-sides at home.

We rode on the engine for an hour one day, thanks to the kind offices of a friend. Perched snugly on the fireman's seat, the supple, sturdy monster, scarcely trembling, except as now and then a fiery breath quiv-ered through his throttle valves, the dust and cinders which had been the bane of our lives in the cars behind, floating entirely out of our atmosphere, we dashed serenely through thirty miles of space as easily as if we were passing the sixty minutes in a home

rocking-chair. (By the way, the happy man who ever
finds a Yankee notion for consuming the dust and
ashes on railway trains will enter into his reward even
in the flesh; blessing, fame and money— I put the
rewards in their proper order of progression — await
him). The wild western dash of speed, the unholy
noise of steam and motion, and the fragile look of the
narrow white track flying before us across the world,
would have alarmed my usually quiet nerves, if I did
not understand my surroundings. The engine was
built at Hinckley & Williams's on Harrison avenue;
the engineer and his assistant were born, one in
Somerville and the other in Lawrence; my companion
was a slim young Bostonian, who could lead a German
or give you the Ottello Fantasie of Ernst one night
and climb Mont Blanc next morning, so I felt perfectly at home. Such a New England crowd would
never go back on me. The gallant fireman, when not
engaged in shoveling coal, explained the country
through which we were passing. "Would n't think,
would you, that that wheat 'u'd be tall enough to hide
a man on horseback next August?" he said. "Its
the truth; I boxed some up 'n' sent it home last year,
for I'm a eastern man myself. My father stands six
foot two in his stockin's, an' 't was taller 'n him.
But ef they kin beat us on corn we've got the
bulge on them in brains. They got to fall back on
us yit."

Indeed, so far we have not been brought in contact
with any really Western people. They all seem to
have drifted here from other places. But they begin

to have mail-boxes at the stations labeled for "the East," so that we feel we are at least drawing nearer the star of empire.

Meantime, we have made up our minds that it is nonsense to talk of the "tiresomeness" of railway travel. Think of the tribulations of our grandmothers in going from New York to Boston! Think of their rough roads and their jolting, draughty carriages, their cold comfort and weary days; then compare it with the indolent, well-warmed, well-lighted entourage of this royal progress, and imagine yourself a martyr—if you dare !

CHAPTER III.

IT is in Missouri that we first come upon Summer and the mule. This much abused but indispensable animal is a feature henceforth in every landscape. Old negroes drive or lead them along stump-lined roads; fat piccaninies shy stones at their patient noses from the door-yards of lowly wayside cabins; gay youths, flannel - shirted and wide - belted, snap long whips as they guide teams drawn by four or six animals over the broad prairies. This and the strange hieroglyphics on the lines of freight-cars we pass, would tell us we were far from home even without the aid of any other moral eccentricity. We are pointed out such landmarks as where the cow-boys raided upon and robbed a train, where Jesse James lies buried in state in his mother's door-yard, or where the spring floods tore their path of desolation through a country side. At one place we passed two young Indians holding a plough, drawn by four horses, at the end of a furrow a full mile long across one unbroken field, set like a picture of Millet against a sunset sky.

The great, bare, desert-like plain of Colorado in the parts through which we pass, forms the dreariest contrast to the green beauty of Kansas. There is scarcely any relief to the desolate outlook. The small settlements are of the most primitive description. The soil

looks baked and caked even in this early spring-time.
A few far-apart clumps of immature, spiritless trees
dot the landscape ; an occasional small stream shows
the prints of countless cattle-hoofs on its muddy banks,
and long reaches of sage-brush and cactus intersperse
the gray country. For heaven's sake, beware of the
cactus! In the gush and enthusiasm of first acquaintance, and as being the only really original thing you
have met since leaving home, you will be tempted at
first to interview it. Take the elder Weller's advice in
regard to widows — " do n't." It looks harmless and
inoffensive enough; it does not flaunt its thorny banner in your faces; it clings lowly and modestly to the
soil and seems to shun observation. But that is all a
dodge to rouse your curiosity. It is, like Bunthorne,
an accursed thing. The most subtly fine cambric
needle is not so delicate as its thread-like spikes;
the most highly tempered steel crowbar is not so
strong. Age cannot wither nor custom stale its infinite prickliness; and a glove of hippopotamus hide
will not save you from its hidden sting. As a specimen of Western ingenuity to show how much vicious-
ness can be put into a small parcel it takes the palm;
it is the infernal machine of the vegetable kingdom.

There is only the heavenly air and jocund sunshine
to mitigate the universal blankness. But when we
stop for breakfast at the little station of La Junta
— which you will please pronounce La Hoonta — so
wonderful is the atmosphere, so invigorating each
delicious breath, that it is like drinking nectar, and
one can be content with the simple boon of living.

This queer little town, which was scarcely born a year ago, and is still, so to speak, in long clothes, is an example of the country's rapidity of growth. Already masons are at work on blocks of stone buildings ; new stores on the main avenue are filled with complete assortments of goods ; neat rows of small wooden houses mark the direction of a dozen different streets ; the clean little station dining-room has copies of Raphael's cherubs and lambrequins of embroidered towels, and there is pure water from an artesian well. By the time you have tasted the different compounds which have been offered under this name since leaving home, you will understand the full force of this last clause. Even after a good strong dose of old cochituate it may be appreciated.

If, in places like this, the store should be only a shanty, ten feet by twelve, do not let your untrained Eastern instincts lead you on a wrong trail of contempt. The owner of one of these infinitesimal trading posts put $550,000 in bank last week after *one* sale of cattle from his back country ranches, — the owner of another could draw a check for quarter of a million, and present it to you without letting his business suffer.

The people look more like the soil than the climate — long, lean and haggard, — a sort of patient, draggled air about the women — an unkempt hairiness about the men. It seems as if an ounce of New England grit would stiffen even back-bones in the country. At one place we passed in the gloaming, last evening, the male population had turned out en

masse at the station, and every individual creature
stood on the platform with the same leg bent at the
same angle, both hands deep in breeches-pocket, pon-
dering, with the same dejected wistfulness through
the smoke of his corn-cob pipe, the volatile spirits of
our party.   They were too far gone in hopelessness
even to smile upon us.

On country roads, in small settlements, and around
station-houses, one is constantly meeting the different
characters of the modern Western drama.   The
"Jedge " of the Danites squirted tobacco juice with
artistic nicety within a hair's breadth of my head at
Emporia.   M'liss looked at us from under her tangled
hair at a cabin door just this side of Las Animas.
" My Partner " walked into the waiting-room at Flor-
ence as if he had mistaken it for the theatre dressing-
room, and Kit with his two "beats " have repeated
themselves until it is fully time to take a farewell per-
formance.   The women nearly all belong to one of
two types : lank, thin-haired, sad-eyed, sun-bonneted
and calico-gowned, while they are still drudges, —
showily dressed, jerky, self-complacent and montagued,
when they wax prosperous and idle.

When the Spanish Peaks first come into sight,
snow-crowned and symmetrical, with a long range behind clothed in that far-away blue mistiness which
ever makes mountains beautiful, one draws a long
breath of surprise and delight.   From some unexplained atmospheric condition, they have the effect of
rising from a deep blue sea, which is a cure for
home-sick eyes.   It is the first glimpse of the natural

loveliness of Colorado. Still further, beyond the Cheyenne Range, the white head of Pike's Peak rises in the still, luminous air.

There is no object in nature so grandly impressive as a range of snow-clad summits. The dream of my life had been to see Mont Blanc, — Mont Blanc with the blue Swiss lakes asleep at its foot, the fair Swiss valleys at rest on its bosom, and the wonderful beauty of the Swiss landscape throwing its soaring majesty into fullest relief. I wonder now whether, if Fortune is ever kind enough to let me look upon it, some thought of the desolate grandeur of these its brother monarchs, rising from the awful calm of their grey plains, will not come like the shadow of a still more imperial state.

Pueblo, where we stop to change cars for the narrow-guage road leading to Denver, is by far the most characteristic town we have met yet. Any of the others might with little change be set down in the early stages of an Eastern settlement, and not be much out of place ; but here the acres of canvas houses, the groups of emigrant wagons and prairie schooners corraled under trees or by streams, the quantities of "dug-outs," where a door surmounted by a bit of thatched roof gives entrance to a tenement hollowed out of the hill-side, and the adobe houses — built Mexican fashion, with large doors and windows opening on an upper balcony — stamp it as belonging to a strange world. Up vistas opening from the sandy plains one sees broad streets flanked by long rows of stone and brick buildings; three or four railways go zigzaging

in as many different directions; the suburbs are full
of large manufacturing interests; it is swarming with
active business crowds; yet ten minutes — five minutes — after you have left, just as five minutes before
reaching it, you cannot believe that anything like
civilization is within a day's ride of the solemn grey
sandy desert, with its clumps of sword-grass and
cactus.

There had been a little dread in looking forward to
the change from the spacious roominess of the Pullman to the contracted quarters of the narrower cars;
but to our great relief we found the ease of the reclin-
ing chairs, which fill the carriages of this road, beyond
anything we had yet used for comfort. One could
sleep, resting horizontally as in a berth, or sit erect, at
will, by simply touching a spring under each seat.
There was another unlooked-for pleasure in the total
absence of dust and ashes during this short ride, that,
added to the pleasant looking forward to a few days'
complete rest at Manitou, made the hours passed in
this way really comfortable.

We had long ago passed the point where self-respect
received any shock from the consciousness of dirty
hands and faces ; we could keep up an air of profound
respectability with grimy smooches mingled despair-
ingly with sunburn and tan on our faces, as if in
mourning for the original virgin white which was once
theirs. We had broadened into the kind of muscular
Christianity which Thoreau believed belonged to true
manhood, and could retain unconsciousness of self and
surroundings under the most desperate straits. This

is one of the liberal uses of travelling. Anyone can be charming and natural and vivacious in a Worth costume and a Queen Anne boudoir; but to be fascinating, and merry, and altogether lovely in a travel-stained dress, a crushed hat and a pair of torn gloves, with soot at the roots of your hair, and patches too big for beauty-spots over all the visible creature—as some of our feminine women managed—that is to be great indeed!

The quality of accommodations provided in these far-away wilds has been a constant surprise; the fare has been uniformly good, plentiful and well-cooked. At the strangest stopping-places, where one would imagine sandwiches and thick coffee to be the extent of resources, we have found a variety always abundant and often luxurious. How they manage such a quantity of fresh supplies would be perplexing, if the number of empty tin cans about each new settlement did not tell the tale. We are beginning to believe the tin can, and its contents, the pioneers of civilization, they make impossibilities possible. Butter and coffee, two of the tests of good living, have been almost invariably excellent; the exceptions, strangely enough, were where one would least look for lapses. We have been somewhat sorry not to find more changes in the bill of fare; one would think that two or three thousand miles of distance might inspire some local differences of *menu*, but steaks and chops, Saratoga potatoes and broiled kidneys, duck and green peas, ice cream and apple-charlotte, follow you in procession from one end of the continent to the other.

There is not much hardship involved in travelling in such company; still an occasional bit of Bohemianism in the shape of a ragout of prairie dog, a sirloin of prairie chicken, an olla podrida of cactus and cream, or a fricassee of horned toads, would be, to say the least, a novelty. There can be nothing extremely wrong in any of these, when giddy Paris dines on horse-flesh and frogs' legs. Shall we pretend to higher standards than French gourmets? There is fortune yet in store for the especial Colorado cuisine.

There was a pleasant little interlude on this same narrow-gauge road. We were brought to a stand on a side-track for half an hour while waiting for the express, which was expressly behind time at this particular point, to pass, while it was so ordained by fate that four companies of United States cavalry, en route for New Mexico and the Indian troubles — going in fact, over the very line we were to take a fortnight later — should be halted on the same siding. We learned a good deal in those thirty minutes of the military feeling in regard to poor Lo. "No good Indian but a dead one," is the whole case in a nutshell. From Commander-in-Chief Sherman to his youngest drummer-boy their voice is all for war, and that a war of extermination. It is plain that there is no other solution than that of force for the present crisis; but this is a poor substitute for a substantial settling of difficulties. There never was and never will be a greater muddle, than our Government have made over the Indian question. These men were bright, brave-looking fellows, young and full of spirit, armed to the teeth, with a dash and abandon that would suit a dime novel hero. A girdle of cartridges in a wide belt around the waist, a villainous double-bladed knife almost as broad as a trowel, a Colt's army revolver, a short musket or rifle—I am not yet well up in military tactics—and a clanging sabre; these were the accoutrements. Add if you please a suit of army blue, a broad slouched hat and a ferocious moustache, a glorious swagger and an erect carriage, and there is your soldier complete. They evidently make light of their errand, and think that a glimpse of a uniform is enough any day to cause a stampede among the Apaches. The pretty girl—pardon, *one* of the pretty girls—of the party held a converzazione with a young corporal which would have passed for a flirtation anywhere else in the world; I don't know the proper name here on the plains. We gave them a rousing Eastern cheer, to which the big boy and a few others added a Harvard "'rah." And then we sank again into the easy-chairs, and tired, dirty, but happy, turned our faces toward "The Garden of the Gods."

CHAPTER IV.

I DO not wonder that the Indians, with the fine poetic appreciation which makes so many of their names eloquent, should have called this place after the great, mysterious, unknown God whom they worshiped—Manitou. The sentimental civilized blunderer, who afterwards modified this by describing it as a garden, made one of the grand mistakes of a lifetime. The impression is of something mighty, unreal and supernatural. Of the gods surely—but the gods of the Norse Walhalla in some of their strange outbursts of wild rage or uncouth playfulness. The beauty-loving divinities of Greece and Rome could have nothing in common with such sublime awkwardness. Jove's ambrosial curls must shake in another Olympia than this. Weird and grotesque, but solemn and awful at the same time, as if one stood on the confines of another world, and soon the veil would be rent which divided them. Words are worse than useless to attempt such a picture. Perhaps if one could live in the shadow of its savage grandeur for months, until his soul were permeated, language would begin to find itself flowing in proper channels, but in the first stupor of astonishment one must only hold his breath. The garden itself, the

holy of holies as most fancy, is not so overpowering
to me as the vast outlying wildness. To pass in
between massive portals of rock, of brilliant terra
cotta red, and enter on a plain miles in extent, covered
in all directions with magnificent isolated masses of
the same striking color, each lifting itself against the
wonderful blue of a Colorado sky with a sharpness of
outline that would shame the fine cutting of an etch-
ing; to find the ground under your feet over the whole
immense surface carpeted with the same rich tint,
underlying arabesques of green and gray, where grass
and mosses have crept; to come upon masses of pale
velvety gray gypsum set now and again as if to make
more effective by contrast the deep red which strikes
the dominant chord of the picture; and always as you
look through or above to catch the stormy billows of
the giant mountain range tossed against the sky, with
the regal snow-crowned massiveness of Pike's Peak
rising over all, is something once seen never to be
forgotten.

Strange, grotesque shapes, mammoth caricatures of
animals, clamber, or crouch, or spring from vantage
points hundreds of feet in air. Here a battlemented
wall is pierced by a round window; there a cluster of
slender spires lift themselves; beyond a leaning tower
slants through the blue air, or a cube as large as a
dwelling-house is balanced on a pivot-like point at the
base, as if a child's strength could upset it. "But
nothin' short of a' earthquake could fetch it," says
the "Doc," our driver, a fine specimen of the Western
type, keen, cool and ruddy. Imagine all this scintil-

lant with color, set under a dazzling sapphire dome, with the silver stems and delicate frondage of young cottonwoods in one space, a strong young hemlock lifting green symmetrical arms from some high rocky cleft in another, or a miniature forest of dwarfed evergreens climbing half way up some craggy pile. This can be told; but the massiveness of sky-piled masonry, the almost infernal mixture of grandeur and grotesqueness, are beyond expression. After the first few moments of wild exclamation points one sinks into an awed silence.

By and by, emerging through another colossal gateway, and following a narrow road built over some abandoned Indian trail, one enters upon the confines of the most romantic, the most unique of all human abiding places, — Glen Eyrie. Fancy this wonderland we have been desecrating by trying to describe, as a vestibule; then an avenue, winding for a mile under trees, with a new vista opening at each instant. At the entrance you pass a little lodge or schoolhouse — a sonnet in architecture, if one may so express it — the small but perfect rendering of a harmonious thought; you cross and recross a rushing, tumbling mountain brook over a dozen different bridges, some rustic, some of masonry, but each a gem in design and fitness; then at last, after the mind is properly tuned, as it were, to perfect accord, the full symphony bursts upon you. In the shadow of the eternal rock, with the wonderful background of mountain, surrounded by all that art can lend nature, is this delicious anachronism of a Queen Anne house, in

sage-green and deep-dull red, with arched balconies
under pointed gables, and carved projections over
mullioned windows, and trellised porches, and stained
glass loopholes, and an avalanche of roofs. It is
bewildering, it is out of place: it is naughty, but it's
so nice. As one of our young men aptly remarked,
" It would be paradise with the right girl."

For a single bit of rugged grandeur the Ute Pass is
facile princeps. Government has widened and built
up the old Indian trail, and now a narrow wagon-road
clings like a thread half way up the precipitous mountain side, a jagged perpendicular wall below, with a
rapid mountain torrent foaming and fretting at its
foot, a jagged perpendicular wall above, with pointed
splintered edges climbing skyward in one bold sweep.
A castle is perched on one airy height; Gog and
Magog look at each other from two prominent opposite
points ; profiles and grotesque outlines are piled upon
each climbing spur until imagination grows palsied
with the strain. Obliged to follow the broken line of
the mountain, the path curves so as at times almost to
turn upon itself, and looking back as your horse winds
slowly up the zigzag passage, you are lost in wonder
and dismay at the temerity which brought you here.
It was up this trail that the Utes, the original "big
injuns" of the country, used to pass to and from their
reservations beyond the mountain and their happy
hunting-grounds in the plains below. It needs little
fancy to see them laden with spoils of the chase or
painted for the war-path, passing in single file through
the sombre ravine which seems theirs by right. At

different points mineral springs of iron, of sulphur, or of magnesia, bubble up as if forced from a siphon, each impregnated with carbonic acid until it effervesces like soda-water. They are the pleasantest mineral waters I ever tasted; the usual flavor of "warm flatirons" being very well masked by the sharpness of the chemical salts; and you will never know what lemonade means, until you have tried it sparkling with this natural champagne.

At last and entirely, you realize now that you have reached a border country. The old Pike's Peak and later Leadville roads, pass in front of the hotel, and at any moment of the day a cavalcade strange to Eastern eyes may be seen passing by. It is Buffalo Bill and his train of Indian scouts, picturesque in broad sombrero and fringed buckskin leggins; or a train of emigrant wagons, household utensils piled in one, stove-pipes fastened to the sides, women and children gathered in the others, and a couple of spare horses, or sometimes a cow, bringing up the rear. A moment ago a long line of pack mules with jingling bells trotted past, a wild-looking muleteer in a high Mexican saddle, on the last, snapping his long whip with a crack like the report of a rifle; and just now a dashing young rider on a beautiful gray mare, with spurs on the heels of his long boots, and saddle-bags flapping at each side of his gallant steed, has flashed up the broad mountain road like a winged arrow. The people ride magnificently, with great daring and unconsciousness, with a pose as if they were part and parcel of the animal they bestride.

Even young girls fly past with an abandon that takes one's breath away, slim, erect, with small jockey hats and plain, well-fitting habits. A pretty girl, I believe, is never so pretty as when on horseback ; but I never knew before how much her dress had to do with her loveliness. The long, sweeping train, covering the flanks of the flying steed with its graceful, pennon-like curve, throws the rounded bust and shapely neck and head into good relief by forming an admirable pendant, and hides the ungracious bend of the knee bent over the pommel. Some of our own pretty maids rode boldly and well, but the awkwardness of the short travelling-dress was too much for even their native grace to conquer, and I was glad to see them dismount.

The horses are all splendid animals; the men would be, if they took as much care of themselves as of their beasts. The village blacksmith is a real study : he walks down the long, red road, his broad trousers tucked into immense cowhides, a wide belt around his massive waist, a flapping brim slouched over his brow, and that swinging, Indian gait, in which all motion seems to spring from the hips. There is an air of jaunty elegance about the straight, stalwart form that is more in keeping with the place than anything else we have seen.

We took two days for a trip to Denver, and from it to Black Hawk and Central City. The view of the mountain range which one gets on this route is enchantingly beautiful. Toward the end the road crosses at such an angle that you see a long line of peaks reaching nearly a hundred miles across the gray plain, and lifting snow-capped summits to the sky till they melt in the far distance. Denver itself is laid out on a most opulent scale, and must be of immense interest to business men. It boasts in its new Opera House, one of the finest theatres in the United States; a little gorgeous in tone, in accordance with Western ideas, but really beautiful and of fine finish. When you see in the windows of the large stores the latest fashion in plush embroideries and Paris fineries; when you ride for two mortal hours behind a pair of swift horses and only pass over one small part of its large territory; when you hear statistics of wealth in banks, mines, smelting works and manufactures that quite upset your slow New England notions, you will begin to realize what this wonderful West is. "East, you talks of things, but here, we does them," said our driver, with the naïve pride of a man who knew which was the better part. The number of men who had made their pile, gone into stocks, got cleaned out, tried again and struck it rich, come back and built a palace, or a church, or a bank, or a block in Denver, was enough to make one's hair stand on end. And this in a place where twenty years ago the redskin and mountain coyote had it all to themselves.

Think of having to come to this city of the plains to find the first waiter who ever was known to refuse a tip! I will not return good for evil by telling where he is. In a place which boasts thirty or forty hotels, some of them with 270 sleeping-rooms, you may take your choice and find him out. But the rara avis belongs in Denver, with its other natural curiosities.

I am tired of saying that this is a wonderful country, yet nothing else relieves one's over-charged feelings. A few miles outside the city, going toward the northwest, is the entrance to Clear Creek Cañon, in which for fifteen or twenty miles the train follows the bed of a mountain brook, through a narrow winding opening not much broader than the width of the rail, at the foot of precipices from 900 to 1,200 feet high. Each spur overlaps the other so desperately, that the track actually writhes in convulsions around the twisted corners. In the entire fifteen miles there are not two hundred feet of straight line, and often, sitting in the central compartment of a train of three cars, we could see the two sturdy puffing little engines in front and the rear car at the same time. As if this were not enough to set one's ideas topsy-turvy, there are a succession of awful tableaux, where nature seems inspired to her grandest efforts, and where a frenzied tumult of wild grandeur forces one to an almost painful climax of attention. The formation of rock, which tends, all through the parts of Colorada we have yet seen, toward an appearance of buttresses and castled crags, runs into a luxuriance of wild and picturesque forms along the entire route. Meantime, you are climbing unconsciously at a rate which brings you three thousand feet higher at the Black Hawk station than where you started four hours before, and you finish by an immense Z up the last mountain-side, which leaves you in Central City quite over the heads of the whole lower world. Anything so wildly trying to the nerves as this last sudden rise

I never felt before. Mt. Washington was dreadful as anything could be, but this was a thousand times worse; for here there was not even a grooved wheel to cling to. It was a plain, bare, every-day track, and a plain, bare, every-day engine, without cogs or cranks, or any other unusual attachment, to brace up a poor lone, lorn woman's faith. When we finally stopped at the little station, it was with a sense of relief which culminated in one deep-concerted sigh. I would not have gone down that incline again, for all the gold in the Bobtail mine over which we were running. There was something unholy in tempting Providence so. And if we did lose our rubbers in climbing down the rocky street through the little mining camp, on our way to meet the train at the lower level, whose business is it but our own? At least we saved peace of mind; and what is temporal loss to spiritual comfort?

There were two days of heavenly weather, after our return to Manitou, and, after that, the deluge. They told us there was no wet weather in Colorado, except at certain seasons. It is true; it never rains; but it pours—sometimes. O how it pours! Yet so heavenly beautiful is the delicious clearness of the atmosphere that unless we felt or heard it we would absolutely not have known there was any rain falling, when it was pouring from above like the sluices of a mill. The soft and lambent air was as fresh and bright as sunshine would have made it in other places. Driving through Colorado Springs one day, that loveliest village of the plain, with the prairie reaching to the horizon on one side, and the climbing mountain range piercing heaven at the other, we had a fascinating experience of the swift changes which belong to these elevated regions. A low cloud of pale luminous gray hid the soaring peaks from sight, and a shadow rested on the nearer side so heavily, that it was stained to deep purple blackness. Suddenly, in one spot, the whelming clouds drifted apart, and in the jagged opening a range of snowy tops kissed the blue sky, glowing with a burst of color which would gladden the saddest heart. I do not wonder that H. H. fell in love with this beautiful place, and lavished the full wealth of her delightful power in singing its praises. It would bankrupt a less-gifted nature even to paint its glories, much less be their interpreter. But we found the old story true, that no one is a prophet among his own people. Our hackman could n't point out her house; he "allowed it was the cottage up thar, but didn't know for sure." Another time, sitting by my window at early morning, while earth seemed wrapped in the soft haze of dreamland, of a sudden the curtain of cloud began to roll from the windows of the deep, intense heaven of blue above it, and the poetry of sunshine—the sunshine of Colorado— blazed with golden glory over the world.

CHAPTER V.

IT was during the first day at Manitou that we made acquaintance with the burros. It is the nightingale of Colorado; its range of voice is limited, consisting indeed of only two .notes; but the amount of eloquence, the superb quality, the deep resonance and flexible sinuosity which can be thrown by this natural musician into such a small compass, is, like everything else here, tremendous. As he lopes down the village street, the larboard ear in air while the starboard droops limply, the long tapir-like nose quivering with the mighty volume of sound which is pouring through it, the sloping Chinese eyes looking at you sideways with the lack-lustre expression of the race, and an artistic kick thrown in occasionally to produce the tremolo which adds the last touch of grace to the singing voice, you are overwhelmed. When its Scriptural namesake spoke to Balaam, he was never more surprised.

We had a vague impression that on striking these high altitudes the ills which flesh is heir to would vanish; but there is, alas! no royal road to health. Even in the upper atmosphere of this rarer, purer world, there are such things as pull-backs. Aside from the difficulty of breathing into which the first plunge dipped most of the party, it seemed for a time to disarrange everything connected with throat and lungs, so that

"Those now coughed who never coughed before,
And those who always coughed now coughed the more."

For a few days it sounded like an out-of-door clinic for throat diseases. But at the same time there was an invigoration, a plenary indulgence of oxygen in every breath, that eased the most profound fatigue in a few minutes. After a walk or a climb that would have made your bones ache for days on that beloved stern and rock-bound coast at home, you would be up and at it again in an hour's time as fresh as a daisy. But the tendency to bronchial trouble placed us all at a disadvantage. The wet weather which came, and I believe went, with us, most unusual at this time of year, may have had something to do with it; but the altitude was the principal factor. When you live and move in the clouds around the head of Mt. Washington, or rather above them, you must expect to pay the piper. But if we had had only pleasant weather, would we have known the fascination of those cloud effects up the billowy mountain sides? Would we have seen them under every possible variation, from thunder to snow, from moonlight to inky blackness? When I looked out that last morning, would the old moon have been sailing her silver boat through the blue zenith, while pale, rosy flames were springing from the horizon upward, touching the snowy mountain peaks with the real Alpine glow? Once, in a ramble to the Cave of the Winds, we were weather-bound for an hour in a lime-burner's hut by the side of the trail, while a furious hail-storm rolled through the cañon, and five minutes after the majestic columns in the Temple of Isis, a thousand feet above our heads, were blazing and glowing, as if under some reflected shower of sunshine. The flying clouds lifted here and there, from peaks and battlements; the inspired air tingled in every vein; the heavenly glow and radiance flashed into your soul,—and ten minutes after you were in the midst of another swift storm of hail, or snow, or rain, as if sunshine never belonged to the world. But little we recked in the safe shelter of the wayside cabin while the fierce fantasy of clouds worked its wild way in the narrow gorge above, and, framed in the ruined lime-kiln opposite, our picturesque young man, never so killing before, in full mountain suit of blouse and knickerbocker, stood like a picture of a blonde Tyrolese jäger in the ruined arch. It was not unusual through these days to have four alternate storms in the course of a single hour, with clear skies between; but, owing to the brilliant rarity of the atmosphere, we were never sure it was raining, until we either felt or actually saw it. And this when it was pouring a ton to the square inch! Another most strange fact was that the peculiar formation of the soil prevented any formation of mud, the roads hardening and deepening in color, till they looked as if laid in red cement. These were both novel features to those who were used to the dreary footing, after a four-days' rain in Boston.

It was here for the first time we saw the magpie, a large bird in half-mourning, alternate black and white.

The Colorado blue-bird, an exquisite little creature, with a bit of the deep sky meshed in his wings, favored us several times in the Garden of the Gods; but we were too early, really, to see or know anything of the birds of the country.

The Beebee House proved to be one of the cleanest, tidiest and most home-like we had seen yet. Its beds were perfection; its rooms clean and tidy; its hotel-clerk a model for his kind in amiability and helpfulness, and its open fireplace, full of blazing logs in each of the large parlors, cheer and comfort itself. But it owned a corps of waiters who ought to be broken in before they were allowed to swing things in such a brazenly, reckless fashion. They had a Rocky Mountain style of flinging plates and dishes, so that one never knew whether they were aimed at one's head or the table, and a jaunty way of tipping over full soup-plates and broiled steak, until you were in tremulous uncertainty as to whether dinner would be an internal or external application. , It was high art, in its way, because they never actually allowed anything to slop over, but of a kind which way-worn travellers could well dispense with.

The men were invariably polite and well-behaved to a degree that struck one in sharp contrast to their uncared-for appearance. We never stepped into an elevator in any house, from the time of leaving Chicago, without having every hat lifted until we left it again. A group of rough, unkempt miners would step into the mud on a bad crossing, in order that your feet might pass dry-shod; and the moment they

were addressed by a woman, their pipes were taken
from the mouth. In Central City, that queer little
above-the-world hole in the clouds, one of our party
entered a small grocery to try and get her muddy
boots cleansed. The proprietor not only provided the
means, but wanted to do all necessary work himself,
and finally left his place uncared for, while he took us
some distance up the street to show where we would
find planks properly laid to avoid the mud. One
somehow hardly looks for this in situations where
the people show themselves so sublimely careless in
small matters.

It was here at Manitou that we saw the original of
that wonder-painting of the Mountain of the Holy
Cross, by Thomas Moran. The English gentleman
who has the happiness of owning it had the rare good
taste to understand that everything else in his home
should be subordinate to this exquisite centre-piece,
so that the house is really only the setting for the
picture. The room in which you find it opens from
the outer air, and is made harmoniously beautiful in
every way. At one side a great alcove, lighted at the
top, throws all the sunshine upon the canvas, while
a gem of a conservatory, hung with heavy festoons
of passion-vines, gorgeous in the greatest wealth of
buds and blossoms, in deep-red color, opens from
the opposite corner. The design of the house is of
the English cottage order, surrounded by a lustrous
green lawn, with a rapid-roaring brook tumbling
through and coming to the foreground under a rustic

bridge.   One has only to step from the wonderwork
inside to the wonderwork without, and each is worthy
of the other.   ,

We left this lovely spot with real regret.   What a
golden summer one might pass in that happy valley
among its kindly and simple people, if fashion did not
rush in with "the season" to spoil it all.   It seems
to have more than its share of the world's blessing.
Such air, such light, such majesty and such sweetness, are more than belong to any one spot.   Not
adieu, but au revoir, to the Garden of the Gods !

The moment one leaves Colorado Springs again on
the way to Pueblo, the same dreadfully uninteresting
country, with the poor, tiny houses that seem so bare
of all life's comforts, appears.   If people had souls
enough to appreciate the air and light which are so
lavishly showered upon them, there might be some
mitigation of the poverty of living, kith and kin, in a
bare board shanty of one or two rooms opening directly on the dry desert of the outer world; but I am
afraid even this little leaven hardly comes to leaven
the great lump of poverty.

Beyond Pueblo the Arkansas widens into a rather
sluggish, muddy stream, pretty in nothing except its
windings and the delicate freshness of cottonwoods
here and there on its banks, which are always newly
lovely to us.   It has, besides, for many miles, a fringe
of fortifications in wonderful perfection, some in perfect cap-a-pie fighting order, some ruined and broken,
but altogether one of the most picturesque and com-

plete pieces of nature's workmanship we have met yet. It seems utterly impossible to believe that the walls and battlements, which appear of such solid masonry, should not have been laid with hands, or that the eye of some human architect did not direct the soaring grace of those lofty towers, or the solemn strength of these long lines of .ramparts. Everywhere the great gray plains, stretching to right and left with sombre deadness of color; everywhere the poor, low houses of adobe or logs, which are part and parcel of the universal monotony! The little dining-stations show in their confusion and bustle the want of proper understanding of the needs of the travelling public; still they furnish plentiful meals and give a fair variety. We have been somewhat spoiled by the lavish luxury of cuisine which the larger hotels have given us; but the healthy appetite which belongs of right to every honest traveller, stands us in good stead, and the blessed boon which we enjoy, of plenty of time, even for toothpicks, makes the plainest bread and meat enjoyable. At first we were absurdly conscious of doing an unusual thing every time we tore off a coupon; now we are beginning to imagine what a delight it would be if we could meet every need of life in the same way, by offering a ticket to buy it off.

Placer is down in our note-books as being the first spot from which can be seen the Sierra Blanca, the highest peak in Colorado, and second highest in the United States. It is also down in my personal memory for having the following unique and extremely

Western tradition, as a grace before meat, over the dining-room door: —

> " In God we trust;
> The rest must pay cash.
> To trust is to bust, —
> To bust is Hell !

NO ⎰ TRUST !
⎱ BUST ! — BEAR THIS IN MIND !"
⎰ HELL !

We saw at Cañon City, just as the mountains began to draw together again for the Grand Cañon of the Arkansas, a gang of convicts at work on the road leading through the valley. The State penitentiary is located here, and convict labor does much in the way of building and opening new thoroughfares. A gaunt figure sat at each end with loaded rifle cocked and aimed at the group of men between. In another moment we had whirled between rocky walls which hid the sinister picture, but its harsh effect lived longer.

Of the Cañon itself, I would rather say not one word, but bow the head in reverent silence before this handiwork of the Lord. But for the sake of the dear eyes at home which may never look upon it, and which still love to follow the steps that have wandered so far from them, I must try to speak. Those who have looked upon its awful grandeur will realize the powerlessness of description. The railroad runs through a deep, narrow passage at the base of opposing and overlapping spurs of mountains, always following the tortuous windings of the stream, which flows between with the same wild swiftness which made Clear Creek Cañon so dreadful to weak nerves. Grown more familiar now, we scarcely notice this headlong rush as cause for dismay; but we cannot grow familiar with the massive wildness of the overhanging cliffs above. Gradually the sweeping peaks rise higher; the rushing river grows deeper and louder; its color changes to a perfect raw sienna, which makes a delightful warm tint in the foreground. The soaring mountains leap more boldly skyward, till they seem to scale the very ramparts of heaven, cleft through their centre of everlasting rock by some stupendous power we can only guess at. Whatever is grandest and wildest in nature, pours itself with prodigious lavishness above and around, until, as the train thunders upon a hanging bridge which spans a deep abyss, the sense of might and awfulness is so heavy on the soul, that it results in a sense of real physical oppression. The roaring of the rapids, intensified by precipices which lift themselves at each side; the solemn shadow thrown even at noonday from those mighty ledges; the stupendous majesty which sweeps you from all familiar things and sets you face to face with the Creator, combine to impress an unearthly feeling of loneliness and awe which remains stamped with the memory of the place forever. In the bit of dazzling blue that showed itself over the high fortress like crags, so high that eyes, as well as spirit, had to soar to reach their summits, two immense eagles went sweeping in airy circles, till they disappeared behind the topmost peak of all. It was the only sign of life which would not have been out of harmony with the solemnity of the spot. A sombre veiling of firs covered the lower levels of the mountains; but above, only the bare, barren rock rose with splintered edges into pinnacles and domes, stained here and there with blackness of age, riven by thunder-bolts, or jeweled with sparkling spray of leaping waterfalls. Even after passing this culminating point there was no anti-climax. As the road and river-bed widen, the heights open here and there, showing still other peaks beyond, but all yet dark and awful. By-and-by a single tree, or a group of cottonwoods, throw their fleecy, silver-stemmed branches like a point of light against the grim background, or a single snow-powdered peak of the Sangre de Cristo rises far away. Constantly changing as the whirling road flies east or west, you get by instants some new picture, until at last, through a sudden cleft, the whole beautiful sunny range rises against the horizon, one rounded, dazzling peak superbly prominent in the centre, — "clothed in white samite, mystic, wonderful." Just as this glorious vision bursts upon your raptured sight, there rushes down through the centre of a gorge in the rocky chain, as sombre as blackened trunks of dead trees and funereal firs can make it, a cascade, a torrent, a perfect avalanche of tender glowing green, where a thick belt of young trees have followed the windings of the mountain-side into the open space below. For hours there is nothing to break the strain produced by this immense manifestation of sublimity: you are obliged to sit in awed and awful silence while it pours in upon overwrought nerves and brain, without, as one of the party aptly remarked, even being able to dam it for awhile and take a rest.

Two hours after leaving Salida, at the end of this over-exciting trip, we were hurled into another, which was, if such a thing could be, even more gloriously terrible. Up the great Continental Divide,* the railroad clambers five thousand feet in a distance of twenty-eight miles, to Marshall's Pass, bearing you from the summer lands below, to the region of eternal ice and snow above. As the crow flies, the distance travelled to the summit would not be over eight miles; the others are taken up in devious twistings and windings backward and forward over the mountain. In the course of the route, you pass over giddy trestles, on the brink of narrow precipices, by the side of weighty, overhanging cliffs, or curving edges of black ravines, rising ever higher and higher, until the sight of the dizzy, swooping valleys make you catch breath hard, and you would gladly weigh a thousand tons, so as to have some effect in balancing the swaying train which so airily spins above them. It was toward evening, and we followed the light upward from one level to another, until just at sunset we emerged on a scene of such unearthly beauty as those who had the blessed fortune of seeing, will never forget. Turning

---

* It may be well here to define some of the terms used in connection with Western mountain scenery, — Mesa: a high table-land or plain between mountains; Divide: a mountain chain separating two sets of table-lands; the Continental Divide, between the Atlantic and Pacific slopes; Cañon: a passage between mountains, winding through the lowest level; Pass: a trail built on the mountain-side through a Cañon; Gorge: the wildest and most precipitous part of a Cañon.

a sharp spur of the mountain, we spun over a trestle-bridge, which took a curve, a climb, and a bound across a deep gorge all at once; and on the instant the sun shone on a line of exquisite peaks melting away in the dim horizon, their snowy summits trans-figured with the last rosy flush of dying day. Far below, purple night shadows were gathering already in deep ravines and narrow passes; while above, the sky was still opalescent with the faint, clear tints which make twilight linger so long in this rare atmos-phere. O, heavenly heights, fair Mountains of the Snow! will we ever again look upon anything so won-derful until we cross the border-land to the Blessed Country, and through the gates ajar see rising in the radiant air the shining hills of Paradise!

In the Veta Pass, which we crossed next day, the same manifestations of grandeur and majesty repeated themselves. In each case, nearly a day spent in crossing the barren plains prepares one for the effect to be produced, and gives the sharpness of contrast to the two opposing scenes. A mirage, which lasted for some hours, gave the idea of blue water at the base of a mountain-chain on the left, which had an exquisite effect in the distance. If this country only had lakes, it would be too dangerously near perfec-tion. The mule-shoe curve, which sweeps up to the higher levels on this new trail, is another blood-curdling experience; but so sure had we grown by this time of the security of our running-gear, that we rode through thirty or forty miles in the cab of the engine. The effect of coming in this way into the mysteries of Toltec Gorge is, to say the least, thrilling. You have something of the glow of an explorer who discovers for the first time some new and beautiful land. I do not wonder any longer, that, simply from the love of this excitement, men should be found willing to brave danger of suffering and death, uplifted beyond ordinary human endurance for the sake of the glow which comes when the secret of some hitherto unknown spot lies unlocked before them. There is one superb moment here, when the engine, after poising like a bird on the extreme edge of a sheer precipice one thousand seven hundred feet deep, turns with a swift leap and buries itself with a noise like ten thousand devils in the blackness of a tunnel, from which it emerges to sweep into the sunlight, hanging to the face of the cliff on top of an awful gorge, whose shattered sides reach the tumbling river below. In another place it passes what appears like the ruins of a heathen temple, its gigantic idols still erect on their pedestals, looking with hideous grotesqueness at the temerity which found them out. The formation of this group of rocks is not dissimilar to that in the Garden of the Gods, except in color.

Our audacity to do and dare grew with what it fed on; after riding inside the engine, we tried riding outside of it. I cannot account for the change which made this possible in a couple of not usually heroic women. Perhaps the stupendous boldness which permeated Nature, the magnificent dash which entered into all she planned and did, the very audacity of her conceptions, may have unconsciously raised our moral

standard and strung us to a pitch that made us
ready for any adventure. Be this as it may, we rode
on the cow-catcher from the Toltec Gorge down to
Antonita, twenty miles away; and when you have
ridden on a cow-catcher down a precipitous, mighty
mountain-side, through gorges and tunnels, under
ledges and crags, around sweeping curves that spin
dizzily through the air, while ten feet before you all
visible foothold seems to end, and the next bound
will launch you into space,—when you have done this,
you have received your baptism of fire so far as
adventure is concerned. You begin then to believe in
the Eternal Fates ; you can afford for the rest of your
life to make a retroussé nose at people who have
only known common-place experiences. The thrill of
exultation which this wild flight through the air produced, especially as night drew on, and only the
meteoric glare of the head-light dissipated the profound shadows through which we passed; the tremendous force of the power behind us, all noise and
fury, contrasted with the tranquil calm of the night,
serene and beautiful, with one pure evening star
gleaming in the clear sky, made a whirl of emotion
which was nearer intoxication than anything else.
When we finally were taken from our perch and
brought into the lighted car, half dazed and tremulous
from the unconscious strain, it was as I imagine it
must be, after drinking champagne, while exhilaration
has still the upper hand of shakiness. After this,
anything short of shooting up a mountain at an angle
of forty-five degrees will be a mere bagatelle. The

future hides what the Yo Semite holds in store; but it is no use to tell us it will ever bring forth anything comparable to that last night in Colorado.

There were some obvious and striking advantages about this riding on the cow-catcher: you escaped dust and smoke, while the open air did away with any unusual sound. There was very little jarring motion; much less than even in the sacred seclusion of the Pullman. Inside the cab it was not so pleasant: a pandemonium of shrieks and groans, as the different levers regulated steam or motion; an odious smell of badly-cooked grease; a sensation of being blinded by red-hot sparks and cinders, or roasted to death by the almost infernal heat; an insecure seat on a high wooden stool, with your modest draperies twisted about you, and a jerky, broken motion like the trotting of a badly-trained horse,—these combine against it; but even here the novelty and delight of the situation easily overcomes them all.

Perhaps it was the mental exhaustion consequent on such a strain, that made us, like Silas Wegg, "drop into poetry" that night, at sight of a charming face among the waiter-girls at the station-hotel, where we stopped for supper. She was a bright little creature, and, I trust, will forgive the doggerel, since it sings the praise of—

THE PRETTY MAID OF ANTONITO.

'Twas in the supper-room at night,
  While waiting for a chance to eat O!
We saw the vision of delight,
  The pretty maid of Antonito!

Her eyes were dark and very bright,
   As if she came from Spain or Quito, —
Her pearly teeth were small and white,
   This bonny maid of Antonito.

Her hair was parted at the side,
   Her step was light as a mosquito,
She had a pretty air of pride,
   This charming maid of Antonito.

We do not know her rightful name,
   Perhaps 't was Jane, perhaps Pepito —
But still we love her just the same,
   The witching maid of Antonito.

If we could pack her in a tin,
   Or roll her in a small paquito,
O would n't we just scoop her in,
   And take her far from Antonito!

She looked so fresh, so pure, so gay,
   So red her lips, her smile so sweet O,
We could not tear ourselves away
   From that fair maid of Antonito.

But where she goes, or what her state,
   If married she or senorita, —
Adois! treat her kindly, Fate!
   The pretty maid of Antonito.

We came back through the Veta Pass in the darkest
midnight ever formed; and just as we were crawling
at a snail's pace up to the highest point, the coupling
between the cars broke. We have grown so used to
terrible risks now, that nothing trivial upsets one;
yet I must confess this spoiled my repose for the
night. To wake at some sudden shock and find that
you are nine thousand three hundred and thirty-five
feet above the sea level and the little house at

home, and that something connected with the machinery of your vehicle has gone to pieces, is not particularly reassuring. When you are conscious that your inalienable rights to life, liberty, and the pursuit of happiness depend upon the welding of a bit of iron, or the strength of a piece of wood, to hear the crack of doom in either of them is inexpressibly chilling, especially when you are up in the air instead of being on terra firma. The system of automatic brakes is brought to such perfection, however, that the train can be stopped, even on the steepest grade, within a distance of twenty-eight feet; and every atom of apparatus connected with cars or engine is subjected to such anxious and constant watchfulness that an accident is very seldom heard of.

Everywhere, except when we struck the mountains, the same barren gray plains, with only cactus and sage-brush, or sparse bunches of buffalo grass and moss, to relieve their monotony. The tiny houses are built either of unpainted logs or adobe, neither of which possess any distinctive coloring. Only the resplendent sky and rich sunshine take the dreariness away. But whenever, far off, the dim blue heights were climbing the horizon, or better still, the snowy peaks shone radiant in the eye of day, there was joy enough to fill the present and lay up fair store for the future.

Before climbing the Raton Pass, which separates Colorado from New Mexico, next morning, we stopped at Trinidad. On the mountain just in front of the station, a castle, so perfect as to be astonishing even in this country of astonishing rock fantasies, rears its battlemented walls and round towers as fairly as if planned by the hand of an architect. A peculiar effect is produced by a tree growing at one point just within the massive portal, which has precisely the shape of a flag raised on a long staff. It looks like a banner flung to the breeze to show that the royal family are at home.

Within the last two days we have passed through and over, five of the grandest and wildest passes in America. I find that the guide-books speak of that of La Veta as overlooking the most beautiful valley; but, to us, the Grand Cañon was supremest, because of the snow-clad peaks in sight. Those radiant heights, lifting themselves in the far, serene distance, have spoiled us for everything else. We found in the gorges some lovely flowers, like white Christmas roses, with bunches of mountain larkspur, and a pretty blossom, half blue, half pink, that ought to be a pet with French milliners. Along the plains were spikes of pale cream-color, like a sweet pea in shape, and golden coreopsis with deep brown hearts; while at Las Vegas the hillsides were covered with English daisies, or something so like the "wee, modest, crimson-tippèt flower," that it would pass for it with any one but a botanist.

We have grown really attached to Colorado: it is fascinating in spite of its barrenness, and progressive in the face of its slowness; for it is awfully slow. Even its crack city of Denver is behind the right Boston time by two good hours.

CHAPTER VI.

THE BORDER LANDS OF ROMANCE.

COMING across the mountains into Raton this morning, we entered the border land of modern romance. In those great plains, through which we have been riding all day, and among the beautiful mountains lying beyond, the fabulous gifts of the blind goddess Fortune have been showered at a rate which has often changed common men, in a few short years, to princes. A kind friend has just brought in a story, like Aladdin's lamp, of how riches poured upon one group of men, poor, unknown, and in no way gifted beyond the clear-headed Eastern foresight which grasps possibilities and makes certainties of them. They bought, almost for nothing, a whole tract of country here, with which to open a colonization scheme, and in the course of development found gold mines, silver mines, coal mines, asphalt, platinum, and heaven knows what of mineral treasure. The land behind and beside these includes millions of acres for stock-raising, river valleys for farming, and — hold your breath while you think of it! — one of the snowy ranges that have snared our hearts forever. Think of the more than imperial magnificence of *owning* one of these connecting links with heaven! The president, who is now in Europe

elaborating his plans, lives royally, not far from the
line of road we travelled to-day, in old Spanish
fashion, with forty horses in his stables; with separate
buildings gathered around inclosed court-yards for
the different uses of his household and guests; with
the wealth of the Incas, and a gorgeous hospitality
like that of the brilliant but unfortunate Ralston.
And a few years ago this Prince Fortunatus was
cutting grass or herding cattle on the plains, with revolvers in his belt to hold at bay marauding Indians,
earning with the sweat of his brow his laborer's pay
of a couple of dollars a day.   Was there ever a more
fanciful fairy story, only that this is real life !

Immense flocks of sheep are coming into range
along the railway line now for the first time, so numerous that it seems in the distance as if the great
plains had been piled in spots with thousands on
thousands of round gray rocks.   They are most commonplace and uninteresting animals it is possible to
conceive, awkward, dust-colored and stupid.   Where
do Schreyer and Verboeckhoven get their models?
What different breeds must pose for those soft-eyed,
soft-fleeced mothers, those tender snowy lambs, those
proud-horned patriarchs of the groups they delight in !
They are watched by shepherds ; but neither are they,
by any means, the ideal creatures.   Bearded like the
pard, mounted like Australian bushwackers, riding
like daredevils, ugly, and I am sorry to say dirty,
they as little resemble the idylic creations of the
French and Italian school as a potato does an apricot.
A certain amount of slovenliness is secretly dear to

the artistic temperament; even rags and tatters can be so well "set" as to produce an effect which good broadcloth could never inspire; but the brutal, greasy, honest frowziness of these sheep-herders, has no more to do with the picturesque, than the sheep they tend. If such "shepherds watched their flocks by night," I wonder if the angel of the Lord would ever have appeared to them.

Now adobe houses come thick and fast; indeed, they are the only habitations to be seen, except when now and again some small town boasts a few un-painted, one-roomed cottages, as saloons or hotel buildings. The perfect level of the plains begins to be broken by undulations and low, scrubby hills, covered with something very like the savins of New England. One bit of ground near Galisteo, for five miles or so, might be put bodily down by the Old Colony Railroad at Braintree, and the oldest inhabitant would never know a change had been made. Even the mountains look like Franconia and the Notch; but still the patches of red earth cropping up here and there are like a continuation of Colorado. By the doors of wayside cabins, swarth groups of Mexicans, darker than mulattoes, the women and children with long, straight, black hair, lounge. We have gotten out of the work-a-day world into one of leisure. Every one looks lazy; there would be bustle enough in one street of the sleepiest Massachusetts village to drive this whole nation frantic.

And here is Las Vegas—you see how the very names begin to grow soft and liquid—with its pretty hotel, the Montezuma, a cross between the Pemberton and Nantasket. It is finished inside, with an eye for the æsthetic that is keener than any we have met since leaving the Hub. The carpets are as nice a bit of color as one need crave ; and, from the patterns of the Kensington embroidered tidies, to the shape of the cups and saucers, all is as it should be. So is the service at table, and particularly grateful after the plate-hurlers of Manitou. There was a piano in the west parlor; a new baby Steinway, one of the loveliest instruments ever touched, and there we had one golden morning. When a violin has breathed into it, by some witchcraft of soul, such tenderness and weirdness and sweetness as draw one's spirit out with every tone that comes from it, and when a piano not only sustains but inspires it, what better gift of the gods can the world give us than to sit in the sunshine and listen.

If you want to know the real luxury of a good wash, travel three thousand miles across the Continent, be steeped in dust and smoke and ashes, live in a trunk and a sleeping-car, let your highest ambition be to keep your face and hands only decently dirty, and then get into one of the warm sulphur-baths at Las Vegas, with a neat handmaid to shampoo your tired head and make you clean, and neat, and wholesome. It is the most absolute revel in the world. You will understand, then, why Greek and Roman built baths of rare and costly marbles, and spent hours each day indulging in gentle dalliance with perfumed waters. The popular belief in the country round about, is that the baths will cure everything but consumption, and the atmosphere will cure that, so there is no chance of dying here, except by accident.

We passed to-day in the Apache Cañon, the scene of a celebrated battle between Mexicans and Confederates during the late war, and the ruins of the earliest church even in this early colony; for we are now in an old, instead of a new, country. It knew a more ancient settlement than ours of the east. Here, nearly a hundred years before the Pilgrim Fathers stepped upon Plymouth rock, the stately Spanish cavalier, Alvar Nuñez, led his company of knightly adventurers and Castilian soldiers through the sun-baked plains in search of hidden treasure. And here long before, a nation of brave, gentle people lived and loved, leaving traces in tradition of laws, customs, and works which sometimes shame the boasted civilization of the present.

Just as the sun was setting behind a dim line of distant mountains, we turned across the plain leading to Santa Fé, and saw the shining dome of the Jesuit's college, which is the most prominent building in the place, reflecting the long, level rays. Soon we were whirling through the wildest maze of tortuous unpaved streets, lost in whirlwinds of dust, crossing a shallow ford of running water in the middle of the highway, and enveloped from head to foot in a mysterious feeling that we have been mixed up with somebody else and are cases of mistaken identity. On the warm air, the Angelus is ringing from the church towers; dark-eyed, sad-looking women are gliding like shadows under the long, white archways which line the street on each side; dogs are barking in wild chorus; soldiers lounging in the green plaza; a world of flat-roofed, blank-walled adobe houses, around and before us; supper is waiting in the dining-room of the Palace Hotel, and we are in the city of the Holy Faith, with a feeling as if we were cats in a strange garret.

It is Sunday; in front of my window, a garden of perhaps three acres, surrounded by high walls of adobe, is divided into checker-like squares by raised banks of earth about two feet high, in order to keep the scarce, precious water on the beds when they are sprinkled. Faint little lines of green show themselves regularly through the baked-looking earth, where the very late early vegetables have started, but they are so faint that they scarcely disturb the deep, brown color. In one place a small patch of currant bushes are in full but rather thriftless condition. Along the side of the wide, dusty road, flat-roofed, one-story houses, all of adobe, still show straight, almost blank walls, only a heavy gate-like door here and there, or the closed wooden shutters of a window, breaking the monotony.

These would seem to be the dreariest of mortal dwelling-places, until you notice through one of the doors, which by chance has been left open, that the little houses are each built around an open square, with a court-yard in the centre, at least in the better · class; this is planted with trees, shrubbery or flowers, so that the inner life is better than the outer. A broad piazza is always in front, enclosed under heavy arches, or supported by wooden posts, throwing the sidewalk into shadow, and making grateful protection from the sun. Up this covered sidewalk has just trotted a little donkey with two Mexicans on his back, their feet almost touching the uneven ground. Down the centre of the dusty road comes a sound of music, and three men with fiddles, playing an opera air, appear at the head of a sad little procession, bringing a dead baby to the grave. Four little dark-eyed boys hold the bier on which rests, in a small open box lined with pink and covered with white lace and flowers, the tiny little waxen figure, while a man walking at the side, carries under his arm the ornamented pink cover which is soon to be fastened down forever. Behind comes a motley group: most of the women in black skirts, with the long, graceful, scarf-like shawl thrown over the head, which seems to be the national costume. One with a gay bonnet and American umbrella looks as out of place as the others would in a Boston street. Grotesque, almost ludicrous, some of our people find it, but, to me, unutterably touching; for it seems as if the yearning hearts even in the first dismal pangs of grief are trying to express outwardly their firm trust that it is not cause for mourning, but joy, since "all is well with the child." Indeed, this is the belief which their Catholic church teaches, and it is beautiful as Faith and Hope can make it. Heaven grant the peace and consolation which conviction brings with it, to the weeping eyes following so longingly the little pink casket!

Now a couple of Pueblo Indians mounted on mustangs dash down the place the little funeral procession has just left. Their rather gaudy rags and gewgaws float behind them; a couple of muskets swing loosely at the side; something is gleaming at each belt; they are talking rapidly with each other as they disappear in a cloud of dust around the nearest corner. Leaning against the adobe walls, groups of swarthy, dark-eyed men lounge or lie in the sun, smoking pipes or cigarettes; at one of the small square windows opening above their heads, a woman's face, with the sad, questioning look which belongs to the people, is looking down. In the street, the shawl about the head is drawn forward and held with the left hand so as to cover the mouth entirely, leaving only the eyes visible. This alone is enough to give an oriental air to the place; a long ruffled skirt of either some bright muslin, or black, like the shawl, completes the costume. There is nothing distinctive about the men's dress, except the broad-brimmed, light-colored hat, which is universal. Just beyond the drowsy street, the gothic walls of the new cathedral, which is slowly being built about the half-ruined, centuries old, adobe building of the early missions, shows its buttresses and arched windows. Here and there, always between high clay walls, patches of verdure show a carefully-tended bit of ground, while one large, shady spot, well covered with trees, marks the outline of Archbishop Almy's celebrated garden. In this, he has demonstrated, by the careful experimenting of many years, that almost every variety of vegetation, from the fruits and flowers of the North to the tropical luxuriance of the South, can be grown in Santa Fé, if irrigation is attended to properly.

A soft summer haze is over everything; even the dogs are silent, and only the church bells break the stillness. Far away the faint, blue mountains rise mistily, piled like clouds, along the horizon; and all between, save for the few prominent cross-crowned church buildings, long, low walls of gray-brown or white adobe, make the flat earth look flatter, until it melts into the baked plains beyond. Every motion that meets the eye, except the two dashing Indians, is lazy and languid, as if hurry had gone out of the world. Pictures of that indolent dolce far niente, loafers couched in perfect bliss, are all about, but they do not look like the seedy beats of our Northern experience; they appear to have a certain right to be lazy. Even the team of twelve oxen crossing the Plaza looks like a bit of still life. It seems out of place to be talking and thinking in English. The soft, musical Spanish, with its graceful gesture and liquid flow, is more in keeping with the earth we are in now; American nasals require too much exertion.

One evening, before leaving the city, we were taken, through the kindness of one of the American residents, to see a Mexican dance. The walk through the dark, crooked streets, stumbling, in utter silence, over still darker sidewalks under the deep arches, was so wierd and ghost-like, that it made odd preparation for a festival scene. The primitive ball, which was a weekly occurrence, was held in the one long, low room of an adobe house, which was entered through the chamber of the master and mistress. A single board around the room for seats, a table in the centre of one side, upon which sat three dark-skinned, wrinkled fiddlers, some tallow candles in tin fastenings high on the walls, and a small counter at one end, made up the furnishing of the place. On one side the men, on the other the women, sat motionless and voiceless. We, from fear of infringing on the etiquette of the place, were profoundly silent also, so that a gathering of deaf mutes could not be quieter. At last a short, swarth man, rising, crossed the room, offered his arm to a partner, and still without a word, took his place upon the floor; three others followed his example, so that a set was formed almost in the position of our quadrilles; the fiddlers struck up an odd but well-timed waltz, and the dancers began a graceful rythmic movement, with so much ease and such just conception of the swaying measure, as was surprising. When we remembered the distorted steps we had often seen danced to the much-abused waltz at home, it was refreshing to see all the performers moving with such delicious languor in slow circles, as if the very spirit of the music were pulsing through them. There were many pretty figures, always timed to the same swaying step, and always performed with the same gentle gravity. The women, except for their lovely, dark Spanish eyes, were decidedly homely, the men little better; but one beautiful Madonna-faced creature showed what the type could be when it reached perfection. The dances all resembled each other, and, in the intervals, refreshments, in the shape of soda and sarsaparilla-waters, with glass dishes of bright-colored bonbons, were handed around. We were treated with great kindness, and were much impressed with the quiet dignity and grace of the people, which seemed so unlike the noisy hilarity of a similar meeting at home. It was in keeping with the slow, quiet, grave world around us.

We had at Wallace, three hours after leaving Santa Fé, our first real introduction to the Indians. They crowded the hotel and railroad platforms, offering small lots of very poor turquoise and native pottery for sale. They always asked three times as much as they intended to take, and would sell the tin bracelets on their very dirty arms, or the silver rings in their very dirty ears, for one or two of the "bits" they coveted so much. I am not sure that they would not have sold themselves and their children if the price was high enough. They were a sharp blow to any preconceived idea of Indian nobility; the features, without being particularly bad, were so wanting in any sort of animation; the petty pride in a paint-streaked face or a gaudy necklace so apparent; the dirt so hideous, both of themselves and their filthy, faded blankets, that one involuntarily shrank from contact. But they had good eyes, good teeth, figures erect as a young sapling, and, where they followed the traditional costume of their race, a certain picturesqueness not yet quite destroyed. You could conceive that there might be among them some young chief worthy to be the friend of Deer Slayer. But as soon as they attempted Christian habiliments and disguised themselves in shop-made coats and trousers, the repulsiveness of their dirty personnel was so exaggerated, that it overcame everything else. You were disgusted, and nothing more. Their chief was a much superior specimen to most of his tribe.

We were in a very perturbed state of mind all that night, from some accounts we had heard of danger from the Navajos farther on, and of the dread of the people of Wallace even of these Pueblos. Their mild stolidity might be only a cloak for some fiendish plot; and when you are in the midst of a 'country which is credited with being in a state of uprising, your nerves toward evening are just in a condition to be worked; so, though common sense in the still small voice of conscience declared the whole thing impossible, we persisted in imagining a war-whoop in every steam-whistle, a night attack in every sudden stop, and instant annihilation lurking in every shadow. But we woke with our scalps on.

El Paso, looked from the cars like another Santa Fé, only more caked and baked, if possible, with mountains like dirt-heaps in the distance. We were all somewhat out of sorts after the sleepless night and dreadfully hot morning which followed it, and the clouds of flying dust and lifeless adobe houses made us still more hippish. But the ride across into old Mexico, in spite of dust, in spite of heat, in spite of bad temper, was one of the most interesting of our lives. Once you had gotten across the rope ferry over the Rio Grande, you were in a bit of Moorish Spain. Before and around you constantly, are narrow,

dusty streets, bordered by low adobe walls, with an
occasional heavy door opening into an inner court-
yard, bright with tall, blossoming oleanders, rising
from amid green shrubbery around a tinkling foun-
tain.   Brown-skinned, bare-armed and bare-legged
figures, in short turic and drawers of white linen,
work among the vines in vineyards surrounded by
high, hot walls; a train of Mexican supply wagons,
blue-bodied and white-capped, shining in the brilliant
sunshine, each drawn by twelve burros, with bells on
their bridles, driven four abreast by a cloud of broad-
hatted, broad-sashed muleteers, comes up some narrow
lane.   We drove along a shady road, arched with
cottonwoods and blossoming locusts; a swift-flowing
canal ran at one side; on the other, a hedge of tall-
spiked·cactus, each prickly rod tipped with one flaming
blossom of glowing scarlet, like Joseph's rod, which
blossomed at the top.   Fields of purple alfalfa, bearded
barley, swaying wheat, acre after acre of vineyard,
stretched on either hand, divided by hedges of osage
orange, or adobe walls surmounted by the flat prairie
cactus we had seen before.   A brown, wrinkled hag,
kneeling on the red earth under a mesquite bush by
the side of a small pool, polished a bright brass kettle,
which glowed like some sacred vessel in the service of
the Sun God.   A train of small burros came winding
down one of the crooked streets between high walls of
adobe, each with two tiny, half-naked, black imps on
its shaggy back.   Aross a field came a shapely young
woman, her bright, dark eyes intensified by a white
scarf thrown over the brow, balancing on her head a

great earthern jar of water, while two little boys at
.her side trotted contentedly on, each bearing two
pails hanging from a primitive yoke resting on the
shoulders.   Behind the wooden bars of a grated
window a group of bronzed baby faces looked gravely
out; under an archway the glowing white walls of a
court-yard showed itself, a hand's-breadth of blue
sky shining above.   Once a young girl, with a brilliant, dark face, held up a glorious bunch of deep-red
roses as we drove past, and, running after the carriage, shyly placed them in my hands, and ran laughing
back to the shelter of the placita.

So it was endlessly: it was the novelty of Santa
Fé intensified tenfold, with a greater compliment of
beauty than Santa Fé ever possessed.   One wanted
to go in and stay for awhile with the grave, courteous,
brown people in the drowsy shade of the arches leading into some quiet placita, with the Angelus bells
coming in pulsing waves of soft sound through the
sultry air.   It seemed as if here, at least, care should
sleep, and the bristling, bustling tumult of life lose
itself in the dolce far niente of summer restfulness.
Fade far away, dreams of ambition!   Melt into thin,
blue air, like the smoke curling slenderly from yon
adobe chimney; what has perplexity, or longing, or
vain desire, or vainer effort, to do with this Land of
the Lotus?   What is life but the calm of passionless
content, and the culmination — the apotheosis — of
laziness!   And what are we but disembodied spirits,
floating in a languid atmosphere of luxurious content,
at peace with ourselves and the world!

There was an irresistible fascination over everything. The Scriptural-looking flat roofs, surrounded
by a low parapet, as if the inhabitants were in the
habit of using them for summer bed-rooms, did more
than any one other feature to give an absolutely
foreign air. Men plowing in high-walled fields, used
a plow made of a pointed piece of wood, fitted with
handles, and drove their oxen by a long thong of hide
fastened to the horns. Existence here was under the
most primitive conditions. Perhaps if one could stay
longer, so as to know them well, this small, slight
people might develop an activity which would change
our first impression; but, so far, the almond-eyed
Chinese, coming in felt shoes and blue pjahma down
the long arcade on the sunny side of the street, looks
the embodiment of purpose and business, compared
with the Mexicans before and after him. Business,
if it is not a mistake to speak of business in connection with affairs here, is conducted in the easiest
way; the ferry crossing the Rio Grande is a flat-boat,
with two ropes at the sides, fastened to pulleys, which
run over a cable stretched from bank to bank. The
tremendously swift current swings it across; a couple
of men with a windlass guide it; it moves somewhat
cumbrously and very slowly, while those on the bank
stand fretting and fuming, waiting their turn. A
bridge across the narrow stream would do ten times
the work, or a boat with proper machinery, but this is
probably why it is n't in use. It would be the entering
wedge toward hurrying up, and your true Mexican
never hurries. Indeed, he has pretty fairly inoculated

his American fellow-citizen: they have never quite become satisfied with the railroad.

I wonder how many of our young people would like to go housekeeping in one of those adobe houses. There is one incalculable blessing, — no stairs. If you want to climb on top of the flat roof over the single story, you must take a ladder. Through the door, in the blank clay wall which fronts the street, a narrow, dark passage, usually whitewashed, leads to the placita, or square central court-yard, on which all the rooms open. The parlor has a print or two on the walls, probably, and a rug or two on the bare, clean, scrubbed floor; possibly, a table with a few books, a couple of wicker-chairs, and a white muslin curtain at the little window. There may be a bowl of Pueblo pottery or a brilliantly-dyed Indian blanket, or a sewing-machine in a corner, but this is unusual and superfluous luxury. The dining-room has its round table and a few simple chairs; the kitchen, its fire-place and mesa; the bedrooms, dark and cool, their small, single, white beds, and nothing else. It is not overwhelming, but it is enough; and their house-keepers do not die of nervous prostration.

The system of irrigation is very simple, but extensive. Earthen ditches conduct the water from the river, from mountain springs, or from artificial reservoirs, through the fields, crossing the roads by means of small wooden conduits, which make abrupt, jerky elevations every few hundred feet. By damming the flow of water at one point, it can be turned into any desired channel, so that every field, no matter how

large, is completely under control. They pretend that
it is a much safer plan than that of depending on
natural means; but, for myself, I believe the rain is
the better watering-pot.

This was all on the Mexican side, in El Paso del
Norte, where the three-barred Mexican flag which
should have floated on its tall staff, but did not, pro-
claimed that we were indeed and truth in a strange
land. Of El Paso itself, the Texan city, we have the
most unpleasant memories of the trip thus far. The
day was insufferably hot; we were not prepared for it;
the streets were a foot deep in powdery dust, which
choked unmercifully; we were still lurkingly and
secretly afraid of the Indians and cowboys, about
whom dreadful people were constantly dropping hints
and innuendoes; we were half sick and wholly tired
from the unwonted temperature; iced lemonade was
twenty-five cents a glass and oranges four for a dollar,
so the bitter cup was full. There is no balm in the
Gilead of travelling which will heal so many ills at
once.

But that bit of Mexico, that oasis which only the
rushing, shining river separated from the dust desert
of Texas, with its green groves of locust and cotton-
wood, its hedges of cactus and mesquite, its bushes
of wild roses, its wavy, delicate greenery! It was all
Morocco. It was only necessary to replace the broad
sombrero with the Moslem fez, and pile the contents
of the wagons on the backs of a caravan of camels.
All sorts of Scriptural and oriental pictures came to
one's mind: the bits of blue sky glowing between

naked white or brown walls; the bare-armed laborers
in loose, white jacket and short trousers; the long,
jingling lines of mules and donkeys creeping lazily up
narrow, sleepy lanes; even the lustrous eyes and
teeth, and the frequent bit of bright or white drapery,
kept up the illusion. The children were the hand-
somest race 1 ever saw in my life, and the straight,
lithe riders, doffing hats as they passed in token of
salutation, had a graceful deference which even their
haughty brothers of the East could not surpass. The
odds for effectiveness and picturesqueness would of
course be in favor of the Bedouin, with his flowing
mantle and Arab steed; but somehow or other, though
there is nothing in life less dignified than a mule,
a Mexican can manage to preserve the illusion of
dignity even with this long-eared animal as his
accessory.

The soft-flowing Spanish names of this part of the
world are another source of novelty to our English
ears, grating yet with the harsh usage they received
in Kansas and the middle West. How can Alamosa,
Antonita, Fra Cristobal, San Diego and Valverde be
anything but lovely? Is a backyard any longer a
backyard when it is a placita? is n't a vulgar shop
removed from all suspicion of vulgarity when it is
changed to la tienda? and ought not all tables to be
made of ormolu or buhl when they become mesas?
But in spite of even this fine bit of sentiment, we were
all heartily glad to start again on our journey, and see
fade behind us into the grey desert from which it had
risen the wall of the house in El Paso, with its twenty-

five bullet marks, where four desperadoes had emptied their revolvers at the sheriff trying to capture them; and the more sinister marks on the door-post across the street where the sheriff in turn had killed three of the men while trying to seize a fourth. Such are the legends that hang like clouds yet, around the rising star of the West.

CHAPTER VII.

THE CITY OF THE ANGELS.

THE best specimen we have seen yet of the traditional Westerner, the man whom Bret Harte created and the world has taken as a type, fearless, dashing, yet gentle, was the sheriff of Santa Fé, who travelled with us for a short time on his way to Missouri to pick up some criminals. He had killed in the course of his different terms of service, and purely as a matter of business, ten men, and was reported to be as absolutely unconcerned in the face of danger as Billy the Kid, a desperado who, before he was shot at the age of twenty, had killed twenty-eight men. Tony carried in his belt a revolver belonging to this same Billy, and took a modest pride in showing it and giving its bloody record. He was a handsome fellow, tall, straight, with fine teeth and large dark eyes, and a shy, awkward smile, which made him look more like an innocent countryman out on a holiday, than the reckless, cool, dare-devil he was. He showered a handful of garnets on one of the young people, as if they were common stones, just as an emperor flings diamonds at Patti; and carried a little package of pretty things to an only sister he was to see on his way, as tenderly as any kind, common-place brother might. He spoke of the Indians in terms of such absolute and undisguised contempt, that we gave the remnants of our fears to the winds, and were honestly sorry when the big, brave, gentle barbarian took his leave at Albuquerque.

Nothing can be more desolately dreadful than the alkali plains of Arizona, unless it be those of California farther on. The poor, sparse vegetation is covered with the same gray dust, so' that it looks like the ghastly form of life with the spirit departed, as one imagines the pallid trees and shadowy shrubs of Dante's inferno. It is a world that might be inhabited by disembodied spirits, whose hopeless eyes wandered aimlessly amid the ghosts of remembered things. The saddest of all sad places! Even the mountains, instead of the titanic spurs and slopes which make New Mexico and Colorado beautiful, were only giant dust heaps, tumbled in inextricable confusion, lovely still, though, with a vague, undefined outline, far-off against the sky. The air had begun to grow more hazy; the sky was a paler blue; the enormous cacti, which look always as if they belonged to some past age of the world, and should have gone out forever with the ichthyosaurus and megetharium, lifted their uncouth ugliness into painful prominence. It is the most unlovely vegetable creation on earth: fleshly, prickly, horrible in its stolid, brutal obstinacy; even its gorgeous flowers do not lessen its repulsiveness. You are filled with wonder to see so fair a blossom on so foul a stem; but that is all: you do not love the stinging monster that bears it any the more. Covered with the shining dust of the plains, so that they seem to spring like abortions of the earth itself, they are more than ever repulsive. I hate the cactus: it looks like the reptile of the vegetable world.

At times one comes upon a perfectly level plain like a white sea, absolutely unrelieved by anything beyond billows of sand stretching to the dim mountains on either hand. At other times, masses of the most wonderful flowers, great ox-eyed daisies, golden coreopsis, fine purple verbena, and a lily-shaped, velvety flower of deep, solid yellow, grew in clusters that would make a city forester wild with envy. We filled the car with stacks of these at each stopping-place, only too glad of some relief from the dreadful, gray monotony outside. In the very midst of all this, on what is called the Sulphur Plains, the most beautiful mirage came and lasted for hours. From a blue sea the mountains rose, their purple peaks reflected to perfection in the clear water; while isolated masses, brown and yellow, full of chrome and umber shadows like the rocks at Nantasket, lifted themselves between. I never dreamed before of such an illusion. One could wonder no longer after this at the hallucination which tempts caravans and wayworn travellers miles out of their way, luring them to death and destruction, to reach the shining waters gleaming so placidly beyond.

At Fort Yuma we met another tribe of Indians, better made, physically, than the Pueblos, taller of stature, more symmetrical, and, except for the hair, a shade less dirty. One fellow, with a leonine mane, massive head, and finely marked features, had a grotesque resemblance to Rubenstein, especially when striding across the platform at 'the depot to offer a wicker-basket full of live quail for sale, he tossed back his long locks with a fine fling of the head. The people seemed aware of their natural advantages and inclined to display them as much as possible ; so that while the Pueblo women covered even the ankles with close wrappings, and held their greasy blankets high around the neck, the matrons of Yuma folded one long piece of brilliant calico straightly around the body, and that was all. It was usually passed under the arms, but sometimes covered one shoulder. Most of the braves, wore one striped garment like an under-vest, and disdained to fret their proud limbs by any other unnecessary muffling. Some of our people looked askance at first, and one dear old lady, tugging at my dress, exclaimed, "Why *can't* they make those awful creatures put on more clothes?" But they decided at last that this severe simplicity of attire was one of the monstrous productions of the country, like the cactus and the sand-plains, and so must be tolerated.

The current of the Colorado, like that of most rivers we had passed lately, was exceedingly swift, and the water, probably on that account, muddy. Still the effect, except when looking directly down, was blue and brilliant, full of dancing lights and pretty, sparkling eddies, which foamed at the foot of the tall cliffs bounding the sides.

Almost immediately after leaving Yuma, we plunged into the desert again. Inexpressibly dreary ; the dead plain, the tufted pine-apple plants, the gray cactus, the skeleton bushes; and always the dim outline of the mountains on either hand, like giant thunder-clouds, adding their wrathful, brooding silence to the sullen scene. It might be Sahara instead of California; yon far-away moving speck a train of dromedaries, with caftaned, slow-pacing Musselmans by their sides; that tufted palm the edge of an oasis. And here, praised be the Fates! Ly the brink cf a muddy water-course, his humped back elevated in a broken arch against the sky, his patient neck bowed abjectly as he lifts it to look at the passing train, is a camel: a real, truly, dust-colored camel! When our picturesque young man, with a bright-colored turban wound around his dusty locks, a Navajo scarf girdling his somewhat slender waist, opens the door and shouts, "Algiers! ten minutes for sherbet and pillauf!" we all smile absently, as if it might have been, even if it is not.

Suddenly, almost without warning, we have left the wastes of sand behind, and are whirling between foot-hills, low and green, almost hemming in the track; the great shadowy mountains, still as grim and dusty as ever, stretch beyond; but between us and them such lovely, smiling valleys, such fields of waving grain, such yellow sweeps of wild mustard, such an infinitely beautiful variation of changeful, harmonious colors! Now and again a sparkling stream of clear, running water; a pretty, small house, with its kitchen gardens stretching in order around the porch; the spire of a tiny village church; a camp of Chinese laborers gathered into a circle of small white tents.

The change is so instantaneous that you wait, watching for the desert to return again. But no; the lovely,
smiling land only broadens and brightens; vineyards
come, and meadows of purple alfalfa; the dooryards
of isolated cottages are glowing with enormous oleanders and spikes of tall white lilies; a man walking
on the track, with his hands full of branches of snow-
ball, tosses them into the car windows as if they were
the commonest things in life. And this within half
an hour, after having passed two long, ghostly days
hemmed in by the awful desolation of the gray desert,
with nor sight nor sound of life save at meal-stations
and water-tanks! It is better than the grand trans-
formation scene in a Christmas pantomime.

It seems quite natural to feast at dinner-time on
spring chickens and fresh peas, with a bouquet of
flowers by each plate; it would seem natural if the
restaurant-waiters floated out in gauzy skirts to the
sound of soft music to attend us. Can this exquisite,
perfumed land be the same, by any law of God or
nature, as the dark and direful place through which
we were journeying before?

Back again come the old landmarks of civilization,
the patent plows and harrows, the thrifty, home-
like look of neatness about dooryard and well-sweep.
In broad fields, husbandmen are already harvesting
some of their crops, while others are just beginning
to spring into the sunshine. Strange-leaved trees,
the deep slaty-blue of the eucalyptus, the generous,
large-armed shade of the walnut, the gigantic, deeply-
scalloped foliage of the fig, come now and again to

vary the landscape. The wayside grass grows tall
and thick, headed like bearded barley; the flowers are
larger; climbing roses festoon the entire fronts of
the little houses, and tangled white honeysuckles rise
like trees into the air. There, a hedge of callas lifts
itself statelily six feet above the garden border; here,
a one-story cottage is covered to the eaves with trailing smilax. We are in constant bewilderment and
ecstasy, until, just as the sun is setting behind the old
belfry of the ancient mission-church of San Gabriel,
and the evening star we have seen so often is rising
with the pale silver bow of the newest of all new moons
by its side, a breath of fragrance unknown before,
an impalpable, fine essence, as of something we have
known in dreams, floats across the still air, and we
know that at last—at last—we have come into the
promised kingdom, and are flying through the orange
groves of the Land of Flowers.

When we rode out next day from Los Angeles to
the Mission, and, after passing miles of spicy avenues,
stretching right and left in long diverging lines of
glossy, dark-leaved trees, white with blossoms on the
outer edges, and heavy with red-gold clusters of fruit
within, turned into the lane leading to Sierra Madre
Villa, it was too utterly beautiful for anything but
fairyland. A beauty as different from that of Manitou
as can well be imagined; warm, voluptuous, languish-
ing beauty; air faint with odors of millions of sleepy
flowers; a bewilderment of bloom and brightness; a
veritable, wild garden, with everything from a timid
New England pink or English violet to the passionate

depth of a forest of jacqueminots, or the stately,
Juno-like waxiness of a catalpa.   Such a riotous
wealth of bloom and fragrance, as if Nature had gone
on a revel, and, tipsy with delight, had spun into
odorous masses of color and light every whim that
crossed her vagabond fancy!   Century plants had
truncated columns thirty feet high in the centre;
Marechal Neils and Gold of Ophir roses, blazing scarlet pomegranate tips, slender Eastern palms with tall,
swaying, fan-like leaves, tangled themselves in a
labyrinth of beauty at every step; and behind, loom-
ing like the shadow of some great veiled fate, the
waiting mountains rose, half hidden by the misty
blue air.

We drove through the most extensive orange groves
and vineyards of the region, and were royally treated.
I wonder whether oranges ever again will taste so
sweet as those great luscious globes; I know they
never will, for while we were eating them there was
the wonderful, half-known world about us, with all its
witchery.   Even if I had them at home,

> " I could not bring back the sea and the sky —
> It sang to the ear; they sang to the eye,"

as Emerson says in one of his loveliest poems.

We are lodged in the dearest and quietest little
house. You pass from the big, bustling, crowded
hotel, through a long corridor into a sunny back street;
you climb a flight of steep, steep steps set in the face
of a wall thirty feet high ; you pass under an archway of cypress into a bit of garden, with heliotrope
bushes higher than your head, banks of geraniums,

beds of cactus, hedges of roses and jessamine, and there you find a little atom of a house, with bay-windows jutting into the flowery wilderness, cool and shady and altogether delightful. A small bit of paradise; still you know the serpent entered even there, so it is not out of the way that we should have private grievance. But worlds would not buy me to mention what.

After a week of Los Angeles, it resolves itself into a sort of hybrid town, with no absolutely distinct point about it, except the always wonderful flowers. In the Spanish quarter, the old adobe houses lose their individuality by having sloping, instead of flat, roofs, and the broad streets take entirely away the hot, tropical effect, which the sun-dried walls had in El Paso and Santa Fé. They look here more like common, small tenement blocks, not dirty enough to be picturesque, nor clean enough to be decent. The children are not so pretty, and the women more slovenly than those we saw before; still, with many lovely faces, the soft, dark eyes always brilliantly beautiful, with a clear olive tint, and a fine oval in the outline. The color in a large majority of the people, however, is quite as black as most negroes; and the contrast between the fineness of the sharp, rather thin features, and decidedly ebon skin, is most marked.

In the main streets, filled with a very Eastern bustle of traffic, the florid style of architecture, adorned with a flimsy Western efflorescence of jig-sawing, and frequently recurring balconies on the second story, give a mongrel aspect to the otherwise home-like street.

The stores are large and spacious, with whatever we have been accustomed to look upon as necessary to comfort and well being in their broad windows ; but with now and then a bit of something strange to make one realize the four thousand miles between us and the sacred intricacies of the dear home city. Outside the meat shops, hang on lines, thin, long strips of what appears to be untanned leather, but is in reality jerked beef drying in the sun. If the whirlwind of flies gathered about do not take it bodily away it will probably appear again on some of our Boston tea tables next winter. Against the doors of vegetable markets, huge strings of dried peppers, red and hot, appeal to the quick Spanish temper, as red and hot as themselves. Festoons of the same lurid vegetable line the walls of every fruit store, while the broad plank sidewalks are covered with cartloads of Northern and Southern fruits. The very finest cherries we ever saw were in profusion, but dear, while lemons and oranges of regal size went begging. Artichokes and cauliflowers seemed to grow on every bush, and there was no limit to the quantity or variety of vegetables of all kinds. At the principal stores the contents appeared to have been turned inside out, so much was piled outside, while wagons with country produce stood on street corners. One small, rather shabby, cross town, New York horse car, ambled through the middle of the main street, but the people seemed averse to it, or to the ten-cent fare, and we never saw many avail themselves of the privilege.

Sometimes in crossing from one principal thoroughfare to another, instead of a side street there would be a flight of steps and a series of long corridors opening on cool court-yards, with splashing fountains in the centre, and tall calla lilies looking at themselves in a circle round the quiet, shadowy basin. It was in this way that we stumbled once upon the Public Library, with a pleasant reading-room and well-filled shelves. We found some illustrated books on Colorado and California, surveys and travel over the very places we had just come across, which seemed like a panorama of our whole journey. Except by some members of our own party, it did not seem to be as well patronized as it deserved; but perhaps this is not the literary season in California.

Down or up the side streets, the dearest little white houses, tiny as children's playthings, made to look like mansions with towers, and bay windows, and what not, stood each in its own little garden, completely covered with creeping and clinging vines. The people are particularly partial to tall cypresses, cut and trimmed in purely conventional forms into great cones, or round flower pots, or square cubes, — the most stilted, unnatural, depressing trees I ever looked at. These are molded into archways, and set in every conceivable spot on the tiny lawns, almost grotesquely disproportioned to the size. Why they should choose, among the many lovely and gracious forms which so crowd this bright world, such a contracted, dyspeptic, funereal form of vegetation, only the law of contraries can answer. Every house has its porch, large or small, where the family sit and work during the long,

pleasant afternoons, under a tangle of sweet honeysuckles and great white roses, that clamber and twist
and leap, like lovers trying to reach their ladies' lat-
tices. And always the strong, sweet perfume of the
orange groves—for lemon blossoms are scentless—
coming and going on the warm air, and making one
desire that all senses might be merged in one, with
the nose of an ancient Roman through which to exercise it. Simply to breathe that indescribable, delicious, balmly air was happiness; i. was enough to
make the city, as its beautiful name implies, of the
Angels.

Down in the Chinese section, which looked as dreary
as the spot devoted to social pariahs of any country
must, we walked once toward evening, and invested
some loose change in a little shop covered with hieroglyphics, and stuffed with barbaric trifles. Very little
that was new to our blasé eyes after Zinn's Parlors;
the same crêpê monsters for pincushions, the same inevitable fans and umbrellas and embroidered silks
and carved ivories, but not, I am sorry to say, the
same modesty in regard to prices. One could afford
to pay something extra, however, for buying from a
real John Chinaman with a gorgeous pigtail, a set
of the most perfect teeth ever given a human, and a
most decided opinion on the crooked mazes of American politics. He mildly but decidedly repelled our
sympathy on the veto question, and declared that " the
S'p'eme Court of United States do p'otect yights of
eve'y citizen ; " and when we ventured to remark that
this was the very head and front of their offending, in

that his people did not become citizens, but made their money here and took it home to the Flowery Land to spend, he gave us a look of pitying contempt from his slanting Chinese eyes and shook his bald head. He pressed upon us with energy, as much energy as a Celestial can manage to devote to earthly things, some little cabalistic boxes of "pent for ladies; ver goot; red—vite"—which we finally made out to be a very fine form of rice-powder of home manufacture, and presumably pure. Judging from the city streets, they must have found a tremendous market for this in Los Angeles, for nearly every white women we met was plastered unmercifully with rouge and pearl powder. This appears to be a trait among all southern nations.

We visited, with a special note of introduction, one of the very largest orange groves within the city limits, where over a hundred acres were taken up with fine, thrifty trees, and warehouses for packing fruit. The proprietor's house, a one-story, flat-roofed adobe building, with immensely broad, white piazzas, set in a pretty, prim flower garden, and running at the back around three sides of an inner placita, was charmingly cool and quiet; a grand piano, with violin and guitar cases near it, and a pile of music on a small table near the door, made the deep-windowed parlor inviting. A bevy of dear little bright-eyed, deep-tinted children, who were tumbling and playing in true baby freedom among the flowers, and racing up and down the long verandas, brought back certain groups around the little house at Green Hill that turned me heartsick for just a moment. A pleasant, woody smell and

hammering close by led us to a cooper's shop, where
the boxes were being made to transport piles of fruit,
gathered from the great orchards beyond, and constantly replenished from loaded wagons. A large
farm-house at cider-making has something of the same
liberality about it; only that apples, for all their ruddy
and russet skins, can never have the opulent tropical
glow of these huge, luscious spheres. In the midst
of his men the master stood, picking and packing
with the rest, his handsome, dark head and patriarchal
beard strikingly like the Apostle Paul in Raphael's
St. Cecilia. The long, stately rows of trees, rounded
and beautiful, for an orange-tree is one of the most
symmetrical in the whole fauna, stretched far into the
distance, and one drove for hours through perfumed,
shady avenues, in a half drowsy state of bliss, which
resembled semi-intoxication. The lavish kind-hearted-
ness of the people crowded us with stacks of flowers
and heaps of choice fruit wherever we went, so that
our rooms at the hotel looked more like a floral holiday
than an every-day world.

Every quarter of the globe appears to be represented in this strangely populated city, but principally
Mexico and Ireland. There was evidence of this in
the cathedral where we heard mass; the priest making
his announcements first in liquid Spanish and afterwards in a pure, sweet Irish brogue. In the day-
school of the Sisters of Charity, more than twenty
countries were represented, and the contrast of black,
white and yellow faces was extremely curious. The
gentle but firm rule of these admirable teachers,

showed to advantage in the good results obtained from such mixed conditions. The children seemed very happy, and sang one or two English school songs with pleasant effect. The house is set in an orange-grove, with a wilderness of flowers immediately about it. A species of gorgeous red lily, glowing in royal clusters of six and eight, on top of each tall stem, the like of which no one had ever seen before, grew here in profusion, and we came home laden with treasures.

I can hardly fancy any one rising to sublimely great things in this soft, seducing atmosphere. One needs more of sting and sharpness from which to work out the fruits of adversity. But on a calm, sunny day, when the Coast Range is showing like luminous blue shadow at the end of the main street, and the nearer foot-hills are glowing softly in green and gold, when the air is redolent with perfume and nature garlanded with flowers, O, if one had only every one she loved about her, how happy she could be in Los Angeles !

Part of an hour by rail takes one to Santa Monica, the Nantasket of Southern California, if you can imagine Nantasket devoid of hurry and bustle and fun, sobered by the beautiful shadow of the mountain, changed by the ultra-marine color of the water, and full always of a thunder of surf which breaks with a strong under-tow over the beach. A lovely old garden near by has the finest specimens of geraniums our people had seen yet, and store galore of such jessamine and pomegranites as can only be met here. It was in another garden, old, too, and exquisite with the wild, willful grace which only time lends to flowers,

that we found fig-trees with the nearly ripe fruit hanging under broad leaves, and small olives just beginning
to form.   We found mineral water there also, healthful and horrible, so that the beautiful country evidently
has another element of future greatness upon which
to fall back.

Through the principal streets, wide and unpaved,
the country people come driving with a team of stout
horses, and a strong beach wagon well filled with
buxom wife and troop of healthy children.   The
women drive as well as the men, with a dash that
seems to belong to the Western climate.   All the
trading of the surrounding country is done here,
which accounts in part for the immense number of
stores of every kind in proportion to the houses.   The
Chinese have, along with their legitimate occupation
of washing, taken up that of market gardening, and
bring, in hand-carts and small wagons, the early
vegetables used by the town people.   There is no
form or variety of these which does not grow to
perfection.   Cauliflowers and artichokes, which are
dainties to us, as well as the entire list of early spring
produce, are piled upon the sidewalks or packed in
the small open stores until they are common as
potatoes.   It looks a little oddly to see the chamber-
maid with a queue and pair of linen pantaloons, or to
hear the cooks chattering in Chinese patois in that
high-spirited manner which belongs to cooks all over
the world.   But they certainly work well, and their
kitchens look neat as new pins.   The people have
the real Californian dislike to the race.   It is com-

plained that they are saucy, untruthful, and exceedingly secretive; harsh to children and intolerant of any call at unusual times. I am afraid, however, that the last two attributes are not confined to Ah Sin or Wah Lee, in the rose-bowered cuisines of Los Angeles, but that they are possessed in full force by their co-laborers of Commonwealth avenue and Beacon street. It is hardly fair to blame one people for the sole possession of the little leaven which leavens the whole lump of humanity. We are still unused to the prejudices of the country, and a little taken aback by the contempt shown the Mongolian on all sides. Small children pull their queues with mighty jerks in the street, or jump on the square toes of their wooden shoes, or fling dust in their faces, with as much unconcern as if they were brazen images instead of ordinary flesh and blood; and any remonstrance on a stranger's part is taken with a pitying shrug for his simplicity, and the reassuring formula, " Why, it's only a Chinaman "! as if that explained everything.

CHAPTER VIII.

A CALIFORNIAN STAGE–RIDE.

WE left Los Angeles toward sunset, and came down the lovely valley between the foot-hills of the Bernardino Range, while the shadow of a great storm-cloud hung about the mountain tops. Here and there in rifts the sunshine fell on yellow fields of wild mustard, and mile after mile of brilliant scarlet and orange cactus blossoms. Tall spikes of white yucca lilies, growing on slim, straight stems like pyramidal clusters of silver candelabra, ten or twenty feet high, added greater novelty to a scene already novel enough, and gave us another glimpse of the resources of California in flowers. Long wisps of a brilliant saffron-colored grass or moss were tangled in the tall sage-bushes, and shone like flame in the low evening light. Besides all this was the inexplicable home-feeling of finding ourselves once more in the cars, vis-à-vis with the old familiar faces. It is extraordinary how great a change has taken place in this regard since we left Boston. Then, the train was the embodiment of discomfort, the necessary evil to be borne for the sake of the good to which it was leading us. But now, no matter how pleasant the stopping-place, nor how great its restful luxury, the cars are emphatically *home*. In them we fall into

those easy lines of least resistance, that gossipy freedom of a common household, that happy unrestraint
which makes the charm of one's ain fireside.   If
familiarity even breeds a little animosity now and
then, it only makes the resemblance greater.   What
would home-life be without an occasional love-spat!
So that altogether this evening was one of tranquil
delight—but the morning made up for it.

The traveller who desires to enter the Yosemite
with his natural dispositions undisturbed by angry
passions, and his receptiveness unspoiled by a rank-
ling sense of injustice, had better by all odds tele-
graph beforehand to the starting-point from the railroad, and have his place taken on the regular stages.
These accommodate, on the Madera route, just twenty-
two persons daily; the remainder wait over for another day, if they are sensible; they take an extra, if
they are fools.   An extra, means crowding and discomfort; it means poor horses, and few of them ; it means
no relays and all sorts of hitches; it means, finally,
taking two days for one day's journey, and wasting
more whip-lash and misusing more Scriptural language
in the course of forty-eight hours, than was ever accomplished in the same time before.   If there is any
other discomfort that can be added to the natural list
of weariness, dust, or mud, it is naturally thrown in as
an extra also, but, for a wonder, without additional
charge ; every other item you pay for.

Probably no party ever entered the trail leading to
the valley under more depressing circumstances than
ours.   The wretched car porter, moved by that ani-

mosity which seems to be the leading principle of his race, roused us, in the midst of a barren, flat plain, absolutely devoid of even a semblance of vegetation, at five, when seven would have done just as well. For fifty miles we passed only an occasional desolate-looking settlement of unpainted wooden shanties, and no other sign of life. Human nature naturally rebels against early rising; the world is at sixes and sevens, like any other housekeeper before nine o'clock in the morning. Even the remarkably good breakfast we found ready at the hotel was not able to soothe our ruffled spirits. Immediately after, we were packed like sardines into a jerky, narrow, old-fashioned wagon, and after creeping ten miles over a plain, with a flume like a gigantic caterpillar sixty miles long, crawling into the mountains at one side of it, the driver cooly informed us that we were to have no change of horses, and were to sleep at Coarse Gold Gulch that night, instead of going through to Clark's. The sting of this injustice rankled in our hearts like a barbed arrow that every jolt of the springless vehicle drove deep and deeper. There was no redress possible, which added insult to injury; and the driver could not be made to understand how much we ought to be pitied, which was the final ounce that broke the camel's back. To one who has a real grievance, there is nothing so annihilating as to have any one else refuse to acknowledge it. To cap the climax, the rain, which we had been laughed at for predicting, began to come down in torrents; and, according to the summer custom, every awning and curtain had been stripped from the carriage some weeks before. Rain on top of a stage-coach is always bad enough; but rain sleeting on unprotected heads and shoulders, whose rightful umbrellas and waterproofs are packed in trunks hundreds of miles away, because their owners have been brow-beaten into believing that they won't need them—aye, there's the rub.

The amount of antagonism the average mind can engender under such circumstances is simply terrific; and, under all this dead weight of temper and turbulence, we were trying to see the Yo Semite. And when the "I told you so" of officious friends came to mind, as it always does in similar conditions, we were as near madness as people usually get.

The much-abused driver, who really had no part in this pretty little quarrel, as he was simply obeying orders, vainly tried to interest us in his patient team: "Them horses know more'n we think for," said he; "they've got their hitches an' feelin's jest like any on us; there's Skylight, that off leader, he's got sech a ambition for goin' that he'll pull the flesh off his bones when there ain't no need on it. Now there's Snowflake wouldn't draw a settin' hen off her nest— Git up, Snowflake! Durn it, hev more spirit! Chub, here, she's a queer 'un; you swar' at her and hit her a clip, an' she jest throws up the sponge; but chirp her up a little and sort o' tickle her, this way, an' she goes for all she's wuth, every time. Yes'm, they've got to be humored jest like you'n me sometimes, an' don't you forgit it." I must do the poor man the tardy justice of saying that he bore our ill-temper with the patience of Job, and was much more lenient than we deserved to find him.

He was a bright, cheery, talkative, small person, full of pleasant quips and cranks, rich in anecdote, and determined always to keep the best foot foremost. It hurt his feelings more than our own, to be obliged to lash his tired animals, but there was no other mode of progression possible. He deserved a better "fare," than our discontented car-load; but Christianity, after eighteen hundred years, has not yet been able to teach her children how to bear imposition without storming, and laying on the shoulders of the wrong man, when they cannot reach the right one, — which is our excuse for sinning against him.

It was only at evening, when a little bit of paradise opened before us, in smooth grain fields level as an English lawn, with a few superb oaks and pines, set singly like the arrangement of a park, and beautiful mountains covered with forests sloping gently down to the edge of a rapid rushing brook, that we became again reconciled to fate. After a plentiful supper, with the very best omelet souflée a Chinese cook ever made, we went out to see a gold and purple sunset blaze over the western summits and fill the east with rosy flushes before the tender lingering twilight folded the broad piazza and small cottage ; and realizing then that we had been spared twenty-six miles more of jerking and jolting, we began to allow ourselves to be sedately happy. The little wooden house was kept by a German family, with seven or eight fair-haired, placid-faced children, who seemed to have preserved

the easy Teutonic formulas of life as perfectly here as
if they were still at home in Deutchland. But it was
not until next night, at Clark's, that we really got into
harmony with the place we were coming to. Under
any other circumstances, it would have been a delight
to go through these lovely spots. The road winds in
a thousand sharp curves around and between the
mountains, fringed with wonderful trees, and at every
moment a fresh vista opens. Exquisite little glades,
green and smooth as a meadow, with groups of shrubbery, round and perfect as art could make them, show
at each turn. Delicate fronds of white lilac, frail
and ethereal as frost flowers and fragrant as orange
blossoms, fill the air with delicious perfume; groups
of tall spray-like yellow roses, called for some obscure
reason leather-brush; clumps of large white dogwood
blossoms, and brilliant clusters of Manzanita, their
vivid maroon velvety stems showing like ribbons
between the fine, small leaves of pale-green ; all these
were arranged as in a pleasant garden, and in most
luxuriant condition.

Between them now and again came a white oak,
the bark ribbed like alligator hide, the magnificent
foliage massed in solid green, or the slender, spray-
like needles of young pines or cedars. The succession
of these lovely vistas and green knolls is as charming
as unexpected, and you realize at last what it is that
has been wanting to the loveliness of the lower country, in which trees have always been small and few.
Gradually as the day wears on, the character of the
landscape changes. The precipices are wilder and

higher; the oaks fewer; enormous pines and cedars, growing constantly larger, usurp the place of all other trees. The undergrowth begins to increase until the ground is covered with one tangled mass; wild flowers disappear; more ruggedness creeps into the beauty; under-branches of trees begin to grow bare and withered, or are covered with fine, bright, yellowish moss. For the last five or six hours one passes through the immense growths of this celebrated country; the trees towering 120, 150, sometimes 200 feet; overhead a solid mass of foliage through which flickering sunlight and dappled shadows fall; while beneath, like vast cathedral aisles, the bare, giant trunks, stretch in every direction. These are the woods which were God's first temples, and in them still lingers the incense breath of prayer and praise.

Clark's is a lovely spot; we drove with a last spurt of our jaded horses and a last rattling crack of the driver's worn-out whip up to the front door, through a drove of three thousand sheep and lambs, which their Chinese herders were trying to force across the Merced. It had the effect of a ship tossing on a restless sea, and was picturesque after we had passed them. But I would as soon not return to our muttons. The pleasant noise of a saw-mill mingles with the rushing river which turns its wheel, and small logs, as logs go here, from four to six feet in diameter, wait their turn in the yard. A pet fawn comes up and slips his slender nose into your hand, as you walk about in the delicious air, stretching your legs after the long, cramped drive; down the long slope the fresh night breeze, half inspiration, half lullaby, comes stealing; the moon climbs across the deep-blue horizon, and we grow to be conscious that the charm of the place is upon us. The house is so built that every room, both above and below stairs, opens on a balcony, which gives a sense of airiness and freedom not often found in finer houses. There are great fireplaces in each of the parlors, full at this time of the year with a glow of blazing logs. I could not shake off a feeling that we were near home, among the White Mountains, in the entrance hall of the Profile House, and that a few hours might bring us back to the people we loved.

The drive from Clark's was a repetition of the best points of the day before. We had glorious weather; a sky like Colorado; an air brilliant and odorous; a succession of wonderful gorges and deep ravines, that kept delight constantly on tiptoe, and a glorious team of six fine horses, with a roomy stage. We had a grizzled Scotchman for a driver, canny and kind,— an old forty-niner, with a get-up like McKee Rankin's in the play,—who knew the pedigree of every head in his stock, and had more yarns about the valley legends than would fill a volume. We listened with great interest to the account of Cocoanut-John, the "nigh leader's" rheumatiz, and Billy T. and Emigrant, the two "Swing's," little peculiarities. It was such a luxury to have that dreadful whip silent, and not feel that Bergh should be telegraphed to on account of the poor worn-out creatures, that our spirits rose to concert pitch.

The curves and precipices grew swifter and steeper;

the beautiful, tall, symmetrical trees, straight as ar-
rows, shot into the air; the swaying stage rocked up
and down dizzy mountain-sides at every gait from a
snail's pace to a mad gallop; we grew, as usual, unconscious of danger, and half inebriated with its
nearness; for the breaking of a trace, the swerving
of a foot, the slipping of a screw, would launch the
whole equipage into space, like a bolt from a cross-
bow. I cannot tell what mental exhilaration takes
possession of one and puts fear so far away that even
those who are cowards by nature lose sight of it; but
respectable people who get out of barges going up
the twenty-foot slope of Green Hill at home, and
would consider it suicide to drive up a higher elevation, cling to their seats here like acrobats, and would
like to urge the flying horses faster!

Suddenly across the clear sapphire of the sky a
long, trailing cloud floated like a white feather toward
the zenith; suddenly, again, another and another came
tumbling upon it, until in less than twenty minutes we
were in the midst of a skurrying mountain-storm of
pelting rain. Beloved people three thousand miles
away who dream of California as a land where the
sun shines without a frown or tear to mar its placid
loveliness for months together, and who are taught to
believe that the wall of the Rocky Mountains inter-
poses a rainless barrier between earth and heaven,
take heed and warning! Bring your rubbers and
your gossamers and your strongest umbrellas; never
go out without them any more than you would in
England; turn a deaf ear to the amiable idiots who
tell you anything to the contrary, and make up your

sensible mind, once for all, that though God certainly *might* make a mountainous country rain-proof, yet He certainly never has ; then you won't come to grief or dampness, and your temper, as well as your travelling suit, will be unspoiled.

It was about two o'clock in the afternoon. We had been travelling for nearly three days through a country of such stupendous wildness and utter desolation as left the soul at once subdued and uplifted. Except at the two little dining-stations, the sheds where horses were changed, and a few small settlements on the flats, there had been no sign of human life or habitation through the entire distance. The sense of isolation from the outer earth was so profound that it seemed as if weeks had elapsed since the shrieking engine had torn its way across the plain at Madera, and left us, untried explorers, at the outer walls of this new world.

At last, after one final, sharp turn, that took even our experience by surprise, we came to the bare edge of a mighty precipice and halted. We were on Inspiration Point. Around us, the pelting rain still poured heavily ; above, the black storm-cloud hung in low folds almost upon the tree tops, but toward the west, its jagged edges were lifted, and a bit of clear sky blazed like a sapphire through dull gray. One shining white cloud floated across this glowing blue, and through it the afternoon sun poured a flood of dazzling light into the Valley! The Valley which was the end of our dreams and hopes, towards which unconsciously our hearts had been turning through all the changes of the long journey, with which we had been blindly comparing every scene that approached sublimity before! Dropped at our very feet, and clothed in such fair proportions of majesty and beauty as made it more a-spiritual joy than an earthly loveliness, it rested, silent and set apart, as if human eyes for the first time beheld it; wrapped in a veil of soft, purple mist, that made it seem, in spite of its nearness, like a vision that would fade while we gazed. In front, El Capitan, erect and fearless, as became the warden of the magic world beyond, lifting its bare, white front three thousand feet in one superb perpendicular line from base to summit; opposite, the soft-falling, swaying foam of the falls bounding nearly a thousand feet through the air before it struck the broken rocks below; beyond the rounded curves of the Three Graces, the sweeping line of the South Dome, and far-away the veiled summit of Cloud's Rest, piled with soft, gray shadows. A broken line of shining water came like a silver thread, showing here and there in the depths of the lovely valley, and broadened into a small mirrored lake almost at our feet below. It was—if I have used the same words before, forgive me—beyond conception and utterance. The sense of solitude, of peace, and of an inspiration which sprang from both was so profound as to be oppressive. Even the most frivolous spirits among us were struck with sudden calm, as if they stood at the portals of some divine mystery, and it was with a feeling almost of relief that we turned away at last, and went zigzaging down the dreadful slope of the dizzy mountain to enter in at the gates below.

CHAPTER IX.

THE VALLEY OF THE GREAT GRIZZLY BEAR.

THE last two miles of the descent into the valley was much the worst bit of trail we had come to in the whole hundred miles of staging. The curves were so desperately abrupt where the Z shaped road turned back upon itself, that the noses of our leaders were actually over the precipice before they could swing themselves around, and a faint, sickening dread that the entire team would follow their noses kept one in a constant state of perturbation. But still, as we looked from one side or the other into the beautiful depths below, the feeling that it was good to be here overwhelmed every other, and it was with a sort of mute admiration that we drove at last up the winding valley road, under boughs still wet and shining from the recent storm. Every stain of dust had been wiped away, and nature was freshly garlanded to greet us. Behind, deep-muttering thunder still went on like salvos of artillery echoing from crag to crag; before, the yellow sunshine sun poured down, casting long shadows across the grass, and weaving rainbows through pale mists which were flying high up in the rocky ramparts. We were in a narrow cleft, between straight walls of pale, gray stone which towered thousands of feet above, cutting the

clear, blue air in myriad forms of domes and spires and
sudden, sharp angles. All sense of proportion is lost
in the immensity of dimension; one becomes stupefied
at last with the blunders made in guessing heights and
distances, and maintains a discreet silence. Glimpses
through the trees, as well as a rushing sound of
waters, proclaim the approach to the Bridal Veil
Falls, and soon the driver halts to allow a nearer view
of the foam-tangled, swaying, snowy cataract, which
bursts like a white fury from the rocks above to the
rocks below. Its muffled roar makes the silence of the
spot only more impressive. The curving road goes
on bending more toward the river, where the rapid
current of the Muscat and its brilliant green color
reminds one of the rapids above Niagara. A bridge
spans the swift stream on the left, where a path leads
toward El Capitan, which looks down still from its
mighty elevation, its giant outline changed now to
that of some waiting Sphinx looking with unseeing
eyes toward the future. At a certain point you are
asked to look at a silhouette of the Wandering Jew
etched on the face of the cliff; but, as a matter of
fact, any healthy imagination can make scores of such
pictures at every new hundred feet of scarred and
weather-beaten wall. As one point fades, another
opens; the snowy summit of Cloud's Rest drops out
of sight behind To-coy-ae; the Three Brothers lift
their heads from under. the shadow of the Great
Chief of the Valley; the Virgin Lung-oo-too-koo-ya
drops her slender pearly tears from her cloud eyrie;
high on the right the Sentinel disputes your path;

while far to the left, his long, bright fleece trailing behind him, the Large Grizzly Bear himself,·the Great Yo Semite, plunges three thousand feet through the air in three mad bounds, and dashes himself to pieces on the rocks beneath. This is the most satisfying of all the wonderful cataracts of this wonderful valley; even its voice is more sonorous and deeper than any in the entire circuit of the hills. Mingled with its constant, deep-mouthed roar come irregular detona· tions like the far-off rattling of musketry, or like the deep recurrent beat of the ocean against a stormy coast, when the under-tow beats broken pebbles about, and the sweeping tide thunders now and again against the great rocks. Twenty times that first night after entering the Valley, I was conscious of that satisfying, omnipresent tone; and, deliciously tossed between sleeping and waking, imagined myself at home in the little house, with a nor'-easter beating the wild Atlantic into fury before the door.

Meantime, as we still drive on, the beautiful emerald river is flowing swiftly through cool, moist meadows by our side, and patches of firs at the base of our fortress walls begin to fall somewhat in shadow. We pass the long, low, white cottage and outbuildings at Cook's, lovely though the spot is, and go on to H. H.'s little cottage by the river up above, to a tiny chamber whose window opens directly on both river and fall. A belt of oaks and alders, shimmering all day above the swift stream, is all that separates you from the lofty peak of Eagle's Rest, down the front of which tumbles the sweeping water-

8

fall. You can sit at your small-paned casement and drink in its beauty from early morn to dewy eve; better, still, you can lie in bed at night and see the silver spangles of moonlight fall in phosphorescent flakes, as it tosses airily downward. The tree that shades your narrow balcony has its roots in the stream, and the eddying, rippling flow fascinates you as a sea-coal fire would on a winter night. The air is thrilling with bird notes and fragrant with sweet-briar and wild jessamine; there are familiar faces on the weather-beaten porch of the small cottage opposite; the world is brimming over with the fresh beauty of May-time, and you are in the heart of the Yo Semite, shut out by its white walls from the tumult and greed and wickedness. Can life offer anything more? Alas for contentment! Could any walls lower than heaven itself shut out love and longing? We sigh, even here, for the clinging arms of the blessed babies.

For the first four days after entering the valley, we took no note of time. It was enough to sit silent and satisfied, and let the wonderment and glory sink into our souls, so that through all aftertime, while time should last for us, there might be some clear, blissful memory of it left. We simply looked and listened. Could any one speak in presence of such a preacher? But we were moved occasionally beyond the power of Christian endurance, at sight of the restless, hurrying, foolish people, who, tired and worn with the long journey to the gates, and untouched by the awful sublimity within, were bent upon "doing" the valley. We grew to hate these words with such exceeding

hatred, as made us desire blindly to behead every one
who uttered them. Wildly rushing from point to point,
up this trail and down that woodpath, here at five in the
morning, and there until six at night, always anxious
and unsatisfied, and tired and footsore, — how we did
pity the foolish virgins who, in grasping for many
things, lost the one only needful! To see the agony,
so poorly hidden behind a sickly smile, on the middle-
aged faces, unused to this kind of grimacing, that went
ambling or cantering by on the patient steeds every
morning! To listen to the doleful, pathetic account of
nerves and feelings after the same faces, with more
agony and less smile, had come back in the evening.
The heroism of Joan of Arc, the self-sacrifice of Flor-
ence Nightingale, the determination of Catherine of
Russia, and the resignation of the women of Lucknow,
all combined and boiled down, are not a circumstance
to the immolation of any woman over forty, who for
the first time in her life, mounts a horse to scale one of
these mountain peaks. She bears the moral scars of
her victory on her face for days. She is afraid of the
horse, she is afraid of the precipices, she is afraid of
herself; heaven and earth seem to be passing away as
she begins to climb, and to have passed altogether
when she begins to descend. Every muscle is wrenched
by the effort to hold back or lean forward; every
nerve is tortured by the strain of enduring and the
dread of horrors to come; the poor farce of a guide a
hundred feet off, with four or five horses between,
being of help, if her animal's fore feet slip or hind feet
stumble over the edge of the trail, is so apparent, and

the idiocy of her ever having made the attempt so
patent, that she would give the world for the relief of
a good cry if she could only get down and have it out.
And all because fashion prescribes a certain mode of
procedure. You may be gifted with good legs and
honest lungs, a sound heart and clear head, but you
must not use them in climbing. It is not according
to Hoyle. They say that you will be tired and lame
and unstrung for days after. But I, I who speak to
you, do give you my word of honor that you will have
three times the physical weariness and five times the
nervous strain after you have done the same thing on
horseback.

I do not speak from experience; no, dear madame.
I speak from observation, which is always a cheaper
and often a wiser teacher. The stories which were
poured into our pitying ears night after night by the
unfortunates who had run the gauntlet were quite
enough to keep any sane woman out of it. We sat
quiet, as I say, for days, until some of the spirit of
the place had entered into us, and then began to walk.
First into the foam and fury at the foot of the Great
Falls, where drenched with spray and wild with exultation, we could be shaken by every falling throb of
the wonderful power before us. Then about the
valley, with a climb here and there for a fern or a leaf
or flower, and a perfect understanding of the times
for lunch and dinner. Then to Mirror Lake, to see
the sun rise over the arch of the rocky wall five thousand feet above, while we followed his reflection in
the cool, placid depths of the water below, and tried

to imagine we saw the double refraction. Then grown bolder, with lunch, knapsack and waterproof—and don't you forget it—strapped on back, to Glacier Point and down again the same day, shaken, tired, but supremely happy. So it went on. We did not see, perhaps, for want of time, as many separate views; we did not have a guide to tell us the name of every boulder we tipped over, or every point we glanced at; but we learned our lessons by heart, as well as eyesight, and those are the teachings remembered longest.

The formation of the valley, inclosed within those lofty walls which drop apart as if some infinite might had cleaved them in twain, and in the rent between set this bit of sylvan beauty, with its stream of living waters, its deep, fragrant meadows and over-arching trees, is something stupendous and terrible. Mighty barriers fill all the horizon, set straightly between earth and heaven; you can scarcely imagine a world outside it. The leaping water-falls pouring over the top of this awful barricade seem as if sprung from some mysterious source; it is only when half-way skyward, on some dizzy mountain-trail, that one sees rising beyond the snowy heights which supply those eternal fountains. But from the floor of the valley there is no hint of anything beyond or above. The narrow strip of sky, full hour by hour of changing cloud effects, paints the grayish-white surface of rock with as many tints as the moonstone. Sometimes it is black as night; sometimes white as snow; sometimes full of a sinister and awful calm; sometimes broken into a thousand shifting bits, which almost

seem to move while one looks at them. The place is
a mine of optical illusions. Lean back against the
sheer wall of El Capitan and look upward : you are
the centre of a semi-circular arch, which seems to
project hundreds of feet above and in front of you.
Cross from the middle, the little strip of land between
the base of the mountains, which looks in all and at
most a few hundred yards, and you will walk a mile
before reaching either side. Try, as I said before, to
guess the height of any one of the peaks, or points,
or waterfalls, and you will sit up all night to be
ashamed of your crooked judgment, unless, like me,
you are wise enough to despise statistics. What good
does it do you to know a thing is three thousand or
six thousand feet high, when you have no more idea
than the man in the moon of how high three or six
thousand feet is ? Of course, I could explain by saying it is fifteen or thirty times as high as——but no,
I will most positively *not* drag Bunker Hill monument
again into the Yo Semite Valley : it has been done too
often already. And if I should give you the entire
table of altitudes set out in fair Arabic numerals, what
better idea would you have of the glory, the grandeur,
the utter wonder, of this entrancing spot? Pictures
have given you some warped impression of its outline. Any school-boy in the country will tell you that
it is nine miles long, and from one to two miles
wide; that its perpendicular walls are nearly a mile
in sheer precipices set around it; that the mountains surrounding average four or six thousand feet,
and that waterfalls burst in tangled skeins of silver

from every crevice of the rock. But neither school-boy nor school-master can·tell you anything more, until your own eyes bring it home at last to your own soul, as I sincerely hope they may.

We stopped at Barnard's hotel, if four little cottages, two by the river-side and two opposite among the rocks, can be called by such a dignified title. The chambers are no bigger than a steamboat state-room; the ceilings are made of cotton cloth; the walls are covered with bright paper, and the floor with a hand's-breadth of carpet; there is a wholesome straw-bed and a feather-pillow, plenty of bed-clothes, and, candor compels me to confess, of mosquitoes. You can have unlimited water and towels on your small washstand, and there is a healthy, hard pine chair, if you desire to sit down. There is no lock on your door, and no key, if there were one; the sun comes by day, and the silent stars peep at night into the hallway, with its open doors at front and back, for the thoroughfare through the house is as open as the grassy path before it. It is primitive as primitive can be, therefore in harmony with the wild nature around it. One sitting-room has been built around the base of a tree ten feet in diameter, whose top waves in the sunshine a hundred and fifty feet above the lowly roof. Whatever fine flavor is needed to make its homely but plentiful fare palatable, is given by the wonderful picture of the swift-flowing river, and the glorious beauty of the great falls outside the windows of the clean, plain dining-room. By and by some vandal will come and buy Mr. Barnard out;

then there will go up a five-story monstrosity of a
fashionable house, with electric bells and set wash-
bowls, hair mattresses and modern airs.   And we will
thank our lucky stars that we came in before the
innovations !

We strolled over the plank-walk laid across the
meadows to-night, in a veritable twilight of the gods,
while day faded slowly up the stupendous heights and
the long-lingering shadows crept close, like dusky
lovers, embracing the beautiful valley.   Coming back
a little later, we saw the full moon rise five times in
fifteen minutes from behind one peak after another.
And, now, one side of the valley lifts mountainous
walls of ebon blackness into the starlit sky, while the
other is shining as in transfiguration; the falls are
radiant as an avalanche of snow; the. river lies like
a sheet of molten silver; while the trees, every leaf
and twig, touched into microscopic distinctness, are
reflected as in a Claude Lorraine mirror.   Serene in
its stern grandeur, with the very soul of solitude at
rest on its lofty battlements, and the cold moonlight
heightening its most awful beauty, it is the picture
I would like to take away in my heart forever of the
Yo Semite.

CHAPTER X.

THE walk to Glacier Point, or rather the climb, for there are not two consecutive steps of level ground in the whole of it with one small exception, was the most brilliant achievement of our lives. We started early in the morning, an hour before the sun had got down into the valley, and thus escaped much of the heat and dust which are so terrific later. The constantly changing path gave a succession of exquisite views as we mounted higher and higher, looking now up, now down the ravine. One by one, familiar landmarks came in sight; one by one others, unknown, appeared beyond them, until the whole mountain cañon was before us with one pale-blue line of summits closing it at either end. The windings of the Merced showed themselves in all their curving beauty, cultivated fields looked like squares on a checker-board, the great herd of horses in the yard behind the stables dwindled to sizes like the animals in a child's ark, and the stables themselves like houses in a toy village. Gradually, behind the Yosemite Fall, which has always looked before as if dropped out of the blue sky, with no tangible earthly foundation, a range of tumbled peaks began to rise which looked, later on, as we stood on the highest point, like a plateau of mountains stretching out to an infinite distance. The winding cavalcade of mounted knights and dames, some brave, some pallid, all a little anxious, passed us near the end while we were munching frozen snow from a crevice in the rocks and enjoying the view from the last turn. I never was so sincerely thankful for anything, in the course of a moderately long life, as that I was not on one of those winged steeds, especially as two or three turned their stupid heads to look over the precipice, as if they were meditating suicide. The path was so hard and steep that I would not at all wonder to see the poor, tired creatures take this easy way of reaching the pleasant pastures below, when it comes to going down.

The last few hundred yards are through a grove of trees, stately and beautiful, with mountain brooks flowing between, and the unpainted walls of a large frame house showing like a welcome in the distance. By this time, although you have become somewhat used to the ascent, and learned the logic of resting for a moment at every dozen steps, the continued strain has begun to tell on the faithful calves which have carried you so nobly, and it is with content deep and inexpressible that you cross through the dining-room of the little house and throw yourself into one of the rocking-chairs on the narrow piazza in front. Such a delicious resting-place, and such a wonderful sight! For you have come, as it were, to the gates of another country than the one left behind. Here is once more that loveliest of all earthly things, a snowy range, stretching on either hand till it fades

in the distance; here is Cloud's Rest, with a floating
veil of trailing gray across it; here is South Dome
rising in tremendous bold majesty, overtopping everything else in its imposing nearness; and here is the
beautiful line of the Nevada and Vernal Falls, showing from this elevation like one continuous sweep of
cataract and rapid, as it tumbles between the trees on
its headlong way down the cañon. The soft haze
which distance weaves about the farther summits gives
a dreamy effect of immense distance, and intensifies
the expression of wonderful distinctness and clearness
in the nearer atmosphere. Far beyond, to the right,
the most beautiful point of the whole, to which they
have given the name of one who so loved God's world
as to be counted one of its prophets, Mt. Starr King
rises; the Little Yosemite fills the middle distance;
and farthest of all, where the faint, remote peaks melt
into the dim horizon, some one shows you where the
Lost Valley rests. How I would like to stay here a
year and a day until I found it again!

A path to the left through the woods, leads to an
overhanging ledge, something like table-rock at Niagara, but on an immense scale, which commands a
view of the entire valley as it lies like a map three
thousand two hundred feet below. A slight iron
balustrade is all that protects the dizzy height; and
leaning far out and over, we hurl great rocks down
only to see them whirled inward and out of sight
before they have fallen half the distance, some under-
current of air scooping them toward the base of the
cliff. A small moving speck, as large as a walnut,

resolves itself through the glasses into a country team passing on the river-road, and the pools running up toward Mirror Lake flash like a necklace of diamonds. One feels as if in the centre of a great silent world, with the first hush of creation yet upon it.

Just behind us sat a quartette of young New York girls, or belles, — every New York young girl is a belle by right divine, I believe, — who, with the un-awed instincts of their race, rattled on in the usual high American key about the merits of their respective bootmakers. They could not quite ignore the scenery, nor could they waste all their time in looking at it, while the preëminence of Louis Quinze or Louis Quatorze, in the matter of French heels, was still undecided. Their innocent babble, which would have been exhilarating in any other place, pointed as it was by punctuation-marks made by the prettiest feet in the world, and charming little bursts of light-hearted confidences, seemed just a little out of place in the broad, serene, magnificent amphitheatre they had chosen to make a shoe-shop of. But there is no accounting for tastes. If some people would rather have French heels and table d'hote on Fifth avenue, to the wild witchery of nature and the sour bread of the Valley inns, why, let them. I'd take the dinner of herbs and the dusty boots any time.

Looking at the South Dome from this point, its bald summit lifted 6,200 feet into the air, a sheer precipice of naked rock on one side for the last thousand feet, it seems absolutely inaccessible. It has been reached, however, by means of a rope, which some first daring

spirit left fastened to a support above, and by steps
cut into the perpendicular cliff, up which the dizzy
climber toils and clings, fastened by other ropes, to
the waist of the guide in front. When we remember
the slight young girl living in the valley below, who
told so simply last night of having twice accomplished
this wonderful feat, a thrill of positive terror shivers
through us. Daughter of one of the pioneer families, living almost from childhood in the shadow of
this awful majesty, it must be that some unknown
strength of love and pride, born of long intimacy with
this wonder world, sustained her slender wrists in that
terrible upward struggle. Ordinary nerves could never
vitalize ordinary muscles to such an extent.

A touching incident which brought the sad tenderness of human interest home even to this wild, remote
spot, which looks in its isolation as if set apart from
the happenings of ordinary life, was related by this
same young girl. One of her sisters had an intimate
friend in one of the two or three neighboring families, which, with their own, make up the entire settlement. There existed between these two an uncommon
union of sentiment and feeling; they explored together
the wildest spots, until every inch of the valley had
been made familiar to their eager eyes; they worked,
studied, and dreamed together, and lived in that un-
selfish devotion so often found between two ardent
girls, and so rarely elsewhere. Gifted beyond their
surroundings, they were the ornament of the little
community, and leaders of every social gathering.
Suddenly, and without seeming cause, one of these

bright, active, healthy lives, weakened and faded; and
before her fair face had been a month under the snow
of her wintry grave, her friend was laid beside her.
It was, except for an infant lost before, the first time
death had come to the valley, and its shadow was still
upon the stricken hearts of its people when we spoke
with them.   In every family within the circle of the
mountain walls, the names of these two dear girls,
coupled as they always were together, was a household
word of love and longing.

We were loth to leave the wonders of this upper
world.   Every instant a new surprise met us in some
view lovelier than the last, and we were annoyed to
find that if properly informed below, we could have
arranged to stay all night on the summit and see the
glories of sunset and sunrise from this eyrie in mid
air.   It would have been like a new heaven and new
earth freshly created for our ravished eyes, but the
conservative policy of the inn-keepers in the valley had
prevented any knowledge of it, so we were obliged
reluctantly to turn our faces downward.   I put the
information here, that later, happier mortals may make
use of it, and think of me when they come into their
kingdom.

We started on the descent, unfortunately, about two
o'clock: the very hottest time of the hottest day of
the year.   The trail was four inches deep with soft,
dry dust; the sun glowed like a carbuncle against the
shining, hot rock into which the path was cut; the
air blew as if from the fiery depths of tophet; our
Alpen stocks would not catch in the light, fluffy,

powdery soil; and we tore with giant strides down the mountain sides, inflamed by turns with heat and admiration, until we were sights to behold. Anything so tremendous as this oven-like temperature it had never been my lot to experience before. The sultriest August dog-day that ever wrapped New England in perspiration was a bit of cool comfort compared to it. Fortunately, there were no lookers-on in Vienna to see our discomfiture. We did not learn until later that sunstroke is unknown in this climate, so that we were tortured by dread as well as discomfort; and two happier people than those who sat at last by the tub near the little spring in the valley, ladling the cool water in handfuls over face and head, it would be hard to meet.

One of the blessings which sometimes come in the guise of misfortunes, kept us in the valley some days longer than we had originally expected, and left us grow into a little closer acquaintance. It is madness to take so severe a trip as that required to get into the Yosemite, without staying there at least a week. Two or three days only to bask in the delight of such a masterpiece of unearthly beauty and then tear one's self away from it for a possible forever, is too tantalizing for human nature to bear with any sort of equanimity. Like Niagara, or other places of like magnificent proportion, it requires time to see things as they really are. It is impossible for days to believe that heights are as lofty, within hundreds of feet, as their actual dimensions. But day by day the stupendous sizes grow while you look at them, and if one

could only remain long enough to shake off outside
ideas of distance, I really believe the summits of those
white climbing walls, bare and inaccessible, mounting
into the still, blue air, would seem at last to reach
heaven.

We had the one day of a thousand in which to leave
this haunting spot, a day so perfect that its very memory is bliss. The large dewdrops were still shimmer--
ing on the grass, for the sun rises on the heights
hours before it strikes the narrow path by the river
below, and the shadows linger till late in the morning.
We had a new driver, and a new team, chief of whom
were Strawberries-an'-Cream, and Nicodemus, and the
way, after one last, long, lingering look from Inspiration Point, and climbing the four miles to the summit ·
beyond, we tore down those mountain passes, was
almost too wild for comfort. We bounded in our
seats like India rubber balls in the hands of an Eastern
juggler; the wretched people inside were tossed and
tumbled until they were bruised from head to foot;
but, like the famous ride of Horace Greeley over
some of these same slopes, our coachman was bound
to get us there on time. " Old Dowse," the other
driver, with six horses, was just ahead of us with five
minutes' start; a stern chase is always a long one,
but our man would have broken our necks and his
own twenty times over before he would have been
two minutes behind his " pard " in getting into port.
It is not the first time we needed a special Providence, and found it, but I trust it may be the last.

We picked a couple of enormous pine cones, six-

teen or eighteen inches long, to take home for the
babies, and would have liked to attempt one of the
snow-plants, those beautiful spires of waxy carmine,
in which leaf, stem and blossom is the same vivid,
intense, transparent color, only that every one assured
us it would be impossible to preserve it. Even if it
were not, it would never be so beautiful again away
from its proper resting-place, so that comforted us.
At Clark's, twenty-five miles away, we made a detour
to reach the big trees, and spent a memorable afternoon looking at those freaks of nature. A ball of
twine, which you unwind for ninety or a hundred feet
to measure one Grizzly Giant, *makes* you believe the
size you can never understand otherwise. The driver
points to a spot a few hundred yards at one side,
where a hand's-breadth seems to have been cut in
another enormous trunk, and tells you that it is
Wawona, through which the coaches drive. It requires
the full force of the solid fact that your twelve-pas-
senger team with its four horses fits easily under the
arch, even with the Big Boy on top, before you begin
to realize that it is possible. To talk of trees thirty
feet in diameter is one thing, to see them another.
The tremendous disproportion between length and
breadth, which makes them even when two hundred
feet in height, look stumpy; the queer, straggling, ugly
foliage, the peculiar color and formation of the three-
foot-thick bark, combine to make them more objects of
curiosity than things of beauty, especially in a country
filled with the exquisite symmetry of the graceful
yellow pine and white oak.

9

They are named for individuals and states. We took off our hats with a Harvard "rah" to imposing old Massachusetts, and did the usual honors of the place in buying bark and bits of wood. They will do to trim the little house by the sea.

From Clark's down to the valley fifty miles beyond, the beautiful wild flowers began again. Such exquisite and delicate things I never saw before. There was one we called the Cashmere Lily for want of a better name, which had on the inside of its creamy petals a spot of rich, deep coloring like the figure in an India shawl. We absolutely revelled in the fragrance and exquisite perfection of these lovely unknown blooms, and for want of better uses, trimmed our old coach until it looked like a marriage-bell. It was not until we struck the hot, dusty line of the lower plain that we really became roused to the discomfort of our situation. In and from the valley there were no longer those useful bits of printed paper inside Russia leather covers, to save us from discomfort; we had got out of the region where Raymond coupons took care of us, and were obliged to take care for ourselves. As a natural consequence we came to grief. I will not speak of our woes beyond one earnest appeal to those who will come here afterward, to make assurance doubly sure that they are given a regular seat in a regular stage, not a place on an extra, nor one that obliges them to ride backward. They'll have to fight and they'll have to struggle, but they must insist; and for Heaven's sake let them not believe anybody, *anybody*, even if they look like dea-

cons and have their hands on the Bible. Lying is as
natural to California as gold mines. Or rather, we
won't call it lying. The imagination of the people
assumes the same proportions as everything else, and
they make false statements without being conscious
of it.

Such a coach-load of draggled and dirty beings as
alighted at that hot little inn at Madera never filled a
stage before. We were copper-colored as Digger
Indians; we were hot (the thermometer was at 116
degrees); we were hungry; we were filthy; it would
take keen eyes to recognize respectable people in
such a group of tramps. What I have always believed in regard to human nature, that it is equal
to great things even when it fails in petty troubles,
proved itself here. We conquered in the strife with
weariness, and had, between opera singing, conun-
drums and stories, a jolly day. If we had rested on
our laurels long enough to have realized how miserably unhappy and unfortunate we were, we would have
died decently rather than have kept up such a struggle; but New England grit, and a little Irish humor
which always comes in as a forlorn hope, bridged us
over. But if every discomfort had been increased an
hundred-fold, if we had been jolted until our poor
flesh were black and blue from head to foot, if we had
been evaporated by heat until only enough mortal
body was left to hold the soul, if we had been broken
and bruised, pestered and tormented up to the farthest
of human endurance, we would bear it all again will-
ingly, joyfully, eagerly, for one glimpse of that en-

chanted valley, resting in its supernal beauty amid the
solitude and silence of the everlasting hills.   For
aches shall pass, and dust and tribulation, but the
memory of that exceeding loveliness will be part of
our lives through all the days of all the years hereafter.   There is really no reason, however, why anyone not a confirmed invalid should not be able to make
the trip with perfect ease, by simply arranging properly at first.

The regular coaches are exceedingly roomy and
hung on good springs; both horses and drivers are
used to their work and go at it earnestly; their roads
are excellently well kept, and clever pieces of engineer-
ing skill; there are good meals to be had on the way,
and clean, comfortable resting-places; and anyone who
dreads the first seventy-five miles of staging in one
day, can divide it on the Madera route by stopping
over night at Coarse-gold Gulch.   If one takes no
extra baggage to make care for themselves and discomfort for everybody else, beyond the indispensable
shawl-strap or hand-satchel; if a light gossamer waterproof and rubbers are kept in a convenient pocket,
whence they can be made available at a moment's
notice; if, above all, they carry with them that happy
disposition to make the best of things and ignore
trifles — without which no one should ever attempt to
travel beyond a horse-car line — they can go to the
Yosemite without any fear of consequences.   There
is neither undue fatigue nor dangerous excitement to
be dreaded; exceeding care has reduced the chances
of accidents to the very smallest proportion; and the

beautiful, wonderful way which leads up through the mountains to the entrance of the valley, fills one with such ever-increasing delight as makes ordinary weariness unfelt. Especially in May, when the rainy season is not yet long enough over to make the country dusty or vegetation parched, and the melting snows on the mountain tops fill the great waterfalls with a mighty overflow, while neither great heat nor great cold are likely to torment the traveller, is the world at its best for making this excursion. But while the short season is available, no tourist should ever leave California without making a desperate effort to avail himself of the wonder and glory for all future time of seeing the Yosemite. It is like quitting London before one has stood within the shadowed aisles of Westminster, or coming back from Italy without having entered within the gates of the Eternal City.

We slept in the berths of the palace-car, rather than in the hot rooms of the hotel — where we got nevertheless an exceedingly good supper — and woke in the morning twenty miles away, with a delicious cool breeze blowing through the windows.

Soon the Sacramento began to roll its muddy current by the side of the road; long reaches of overflowed meadow-land, with ruminant kine knee-deep in cool waters, and large, lovely white herons flapping on slow pinions over the trees, to their nests in the tall reeds, made the landscape picturesque to our unused eyes. On the opposite side, far away, Mount Diablo rose. Yellow lupin blossoms for the first time made the land beautiful. Indeed, the prevailing color of the wild flowers through the whole of California is yellow, as if the golden treasure below painted with its own tint the delicate petals that lift themselves into the sunshine above it. Among their roses, too, the Marechal Neil and Gold of Ophir transcend all the others in regal magnificence of size and beauty. We were obliged to put on warm wraps and shut out the draughts, so soon does this strange air change. We were nearing San Francisco.

CHAPTER XI.

THE same immensity which seems to pervade nature in California, the amplitude of resource which bears visible fruit in the magnitude of her people's conceptions and ideas, shows itself down even to such small affairs as billheads and sidewalk posters. The depot in Oakland, which is really the San Francisco terminus of the Central Pacific, coming either from the North or South, is one of these immense growths. For size, brightness, and airiness, it is a model structure; but I think the gigantic cartoons upon its walls, the massive oil-paintings setting forth the superior virtues of Domestic sewing-machines or Clark's cotton, of this haberdasher, or that cigarmaker, impressed us more than the building itself. To see such a blooming waste of brilliant color and gorgeous framing expended on legitimate advertising rather took one's breath away. We had never seen its like before, except for the side-shows of a circus. To the traveller who comes across country by the direct overland route, and makes his début, as it were, here, it must be even more startling, for we had become by this time accustomed to Californian idiosyncracies.

I can easily imagine the approach to San Francisco

across the bay, a most beautiful one at certain seasons
of the year. It is always impressive, as a great city
set on hills and surrounded by water must ever be ;
but when the welcome rains have brought with them
verdure and bloom, so that the lovely world is new-
born to its birthright of fresher loveliness, it must be
a rare sight. When one comes from the desperate
cold of an Eastern winter, and crossing the Rockies
between walls of snow fifteen or twenty feet deep,
comes into this land of flowers, and steams across the
waters of the Pacific to the gates of this golden city,
it must be like entering paradise. Just now, it is more
like purgatory. Although only two months of the dry
season are over, the hills are gray, the streets windy
and forlorn, whirlwinds of dust rush and rise at every
corner, and the first aspect is almost one of desolation. Unconsciously, the Eastern mind makes San
Francisco the representative of California. It absorbs
its interests, it upholds its pride, it is the blossom of
its civilization, just as Rome is of Italy or Paris of
France. Unconsciously, also, people who are not old
travellers measure that part of the world in which
they happen to find themselves, by home standards.
Remembering the glory of June in New-England, its
sweetness, its beauty, its tenderness of unfolding life;
remembering, too, the dreams we have dreamed, and
stories we have heard, of the opulent wealth of this
Western land, the first feeling is one of unreasoning
disappointment. You are ready to be charmed, and
find yourself chilled instead. Although in a vague
way you have heard before that there are such things

as drawbacks of climate and want of finish, imagination, working with what it had to feed on· in lower California, has built up a world of its own and resents the levelling processes of sober fact. It insists on this being the culminating point.

The city is the most tantalizing of all we have yet "struck," according to the Western phrase. Its people regard it with such an absorbing love, and the Easterners who have lived in it for any time acquire such devotion for it, that one expects to be fascinated at the first glance. But one most decidedly is not. All that you have heard or read of the glorious climate of California, the poetic imagery that clings about the Golden Gate, the fabulous stories of wealth and splendor, the songs of Joaquin Miller and the sketches of Bret Harte, clusters about this spot before you reach it, as the Mecca of the Forty-niners. But when you come, tired and dusty from the long overland ride, across the Oakland ferry, and land at the foot of Market street, in a world that seems more dusty than ever; when you see the queer conglomeration of splendor and smallness in even the principal thoroughfares ; when your eyes are greeted wherever they turn by the outlying sand-hills, whose shifting favors are momently sifted over the entire city, you begin to hesitate, and she who hesitates is lost. When, added to this, you find that the gorgeous sunshine of which you have been told so much does not put in an appearance for three days running; that a fog, thick enough to cut in slices and send away by Wells & Fargo's omnipresent express, drifts in every day and all day long; that you must wear your winter furs and thickest flannels in June, while your pretty fluffy muslins and light ribbons are remanded to the darkness and crushing of the trunk; that your crimps straighten out in the most deplorable fashion, and you have to put up an umbrella to save your hat; that gritty whirlwinds of sand get into hair, eyes and mouth, till you feel like a nutmeg-grater, while in spite of all this you are required to indorse the pretty fiction that the world is just as it should be, and this ridiculous city the very choice gem of it, why, it's simply too much.

You rage and storm for awhile; you sigh over your best black satin, ruined after a week's promenading; you sneer at the women in the streets wearing sealskin sacques down to their ankles and white summer hats at the same time; you ridicule the "bits" which take the place of honest quarter and half dollars; the enormous size of everything, from the Palace Hotel to the sidewalk advertisements; the planked streets and universal bay-windows; the quantity of jig-sawing which shocks your æsthetic principles by its lavish out-door application. A few of the bonanza kings are pointed out, men shown to the world by the fierce light which beats upon a throne upheld by millions, and you sneer more than ever. Better the dinner of herbs a thousand times than such a feast of stalled ox as this.

But at last, one comparatively fine morning you get on the dummy to ride up California street, and you experience a change of heat, swift, sudden and lasting. The little quiet monster that whisks you up and pulls you down the perpendicular hills, with a sudden ærial flight like an elevator, may have something to do with your conversion; the brilliant glow of sunshine falling on Mt. Diablo and the blue waters ebbing through the Golden Gate have more. You pass the wonderful houses with mosques and minarets, with conservatories and porte-cocheres, with stone garden-walls that cost a hundred and fifty thousand dollars, with that gorgeous air of having been built regardless of everything save a certáin mammoth desire for comfort and luxury which never struck your conservative New England senses before. You pass other houses, by scores and hundreds, wonderful, too, in a different way, for the air of brightness and perfume of the glowing little beds of flowers around the small tenement, and the general well-to-do effect it gives the places. You hear that at Christmas time, when the cold is pinching the soul through the body by the Eastern sea, the same flowers will be blooming in the same gardens, and the air will be just what it is to-day, and no more; with the added luxury of a daily rain to allay the indomitable dust. You drive out to the pretty park and find that the strange nondescript pavements let your carriage roll easily; that the city has a conservatory which palsies your preconceived ideas of. magnificence; that the fight between mind and matter is going on indefatigably and unceasingly, so that every day sees an inch or two more of sand-waste reclaimed from the desert and made to blossom like the rose—and so from melting somewhat along the edges, you begin to thaw entirely. By-and-by you begin to meet the people, — the heart-

whole, generous people, who take your hand with a
grip that means something, and put themselves and
their treasures at your feet with a remnant of the
old Spanish courtesy which made the days of Castilian chivalry so delightful. You find parlors filled
with as perfect and exquisite taste as any of the dear
Queen Anne houses of the Eastern empire ; you find
pictures whose reputation has reached other lands,
and young people refined and well-bred, with whatever grace culture can lend to the means which make
culture useful. Over and over again you are surprised and delighted at the difference between interior
and exterior life, as the prickly burr of the chestnut
hides the sweet meat within. It is the old story of
Beauty and the Beast; you have only to wait a little,
and look with kindly, unbiassed eyes, to find the fairy
prince under the coarse husk of many an unprepos-
sessing personnel.

But the perverse climate, which is the bane of the
town at this time of year, puts to flight any desire to
yield entirely to the seductions of the spot. After
the few morning hours, there is a chilliness constantly
in the air, modelled on the worst form of the east
winds which are our bane at home. The fog, which
would be called fine rain in any other place where
good English was spoken, is· of almost daily occurrence ; and the change between the sunny and shady
side of the street, at the same instant of time, is something truly western in dimensions. Besides, you don't
believe, and don't want to believe, in a country where
a woman cannot add to her armory of legitimate

weapons such telling and trenchant properties as summer dresses, airy, fresh and elegant. Think of having no change of base, but fighting it out on a winter line all summer. What chance is there for a glorious campaign under such conditions?

We have had as yet in this first week only a preliminary or bird's-eye view. It will take much longer time to develop the real state of things here, and how it compares with those of other places. The trouble is, in short trips, that one rarely gets beyond the simple first glance. It is like standing on a mountain side; distance hides all the lesser inequalities and makes the world look as if on a dead level. Just as in meeting human acquaintances, all the little individualities come out afterward.

Once you have driven through the Golden Gate Park on the way to the Cliff House, and seen the manner in which the pushing sand-hills toss and tumble up from the sea, whelming trees and flowers in their way, you will never again wonder that they have so much dust in San Francisco; the surprise will be that they have so little, for the entire place is built on a sandbank. It is almost a miracle to see the masses of fragrant yellow lupin, which is their first agent in reclaiming this shifting waste, striking root and bearing brilliant spikes of blossoms and luxuriant foliage on so frail a foundation. It looks as if at any moment, like a scene at a theatre, it might be pushed out of sight and the wild ocean claim its own again.

This park proves conclusively, like the Archbishop's garden at Santa Fé, what an adequate system of watering could do for the rest of the city. It is placed in the most desperately barren spot of all, where the yellow sand is blown in huge billows, and threatens to overflow everything; yet patience, and time, and pure water, three of the best things in God's world, and most easily in every one's reach, have made the spot in a couple of years green as an emerald and a real delight to the eyes. We could not help wishing that some time or other a Crystal Palace, some miniature edition of their beautiful conservatory, might make our own Royal Pleasure Garden complete by giving us a bit of brightness in winter-time. These Californian people do not need conservatories. The poorest of them is a nabob in the matter of flowers. Along the street, men and boys by the dozen offer you huge bouquets of jacqueminots or great bunches of assorted flowers for ten cents; in the bits of gardens outside every house, there are blossoms the whole year round, and the passer-by can feast his senses on perfume and brightness from New Year's day to Christmas. But here, where for five or six months we have the harshness of winter outside, with no atom of color to relieve the gray or white monotone, how more than delicious it would be to step within transparent walls and welcome the bloom of summer back again. Now that the dear little city is stretching her arms upward and outward in search of jewels to adorn her, why doesn't some one of her generous children celebrate his loving remembrance by a perpetual fellowship of flowers? It would be better than all the windows in Memorial Hall.

The longer one stays here the longer one wants to stay. By the time a second week is passing, one begins to see something of the inner life and motive which causes much of the outer expression. For instance, the absurdity, as it seems in the first place, of building these elegant mansions, veritable Chateaux en Espagne, of wood, is explained by the extreme difficulty of procuring stone, and still more by the always present dread of earthquakes. Although the people profess to laugh at these little climatic outbursts of fever and ague, there is still deep down in their hearts a nervous and unexpressed dread of what may happen. They say, and truly, that lightning kills more people in one year in the East, than their earthquakes have, all massed together, since time immemorial; but that does not get rid of the fact, that any time of any year one single tremendous shake may bring with it a sweeping storm of destruction. Every one who has ever felt even the slightest shock agrees in declaring that the helpless horror of the situation is beyond that caused by any other natural agent; and even men used to similar manifestations all their lives, turn pale at each new one. The question of expense, which seems naturally to be a secondary one in this land of magnificent fortunes, yet holds for something, when a palace that has cost half a million, in its present material, would mount to three millions in more substantial form. There must be a limit; and, though the air is thick with fortunes of thousands and hundreds of thousands, still millions do not hang on every bush even in California.

CHAPTER XII.

THE three or four days we spent at Monterey, while still having our headquarters at San Francisco, made altogether the pleasantest memory we had of California. The place itself is hard to classify, because of its exceeding loveliness. We have nothing at home that approaches the exquisite setting of this exquisite house, a summer hotel prettier even than the Montezuma at Las Vegas, and in an adorable spot, so far as nature is concerned. The pretty, quaint old town lying near by, on the shore of a quiet harbor, makes an admirable site for research, amid its adobe houses and ruined missions; but it is the Del Monte hotel particularly which has become now an objective point for tourists. The Pacific, all along this coast, wears constantly that dazzling sapphire blue which we see at home only at special times; the sky carries out the same superb color with a glow and depth of sunshine super-added, which is almost too brilliant for belief; and a series of curving beaches of shining, snowy, white sand, are covered here and there, even down to the water's edge, by a growth of the most picturesque trees on this continent. These are a species of flat-topped, sombre-leaved cypresses, with gnarled and twisted

10

trunks, bent into all sorts of impossible shapes, making
the most weird and striking picture, and compensating
in their dense shadows for the glowing beauty of sea
and sky beyond. They are, I believe, unique. to this
locality, and remind one constantly of those weird
cedars of the Roman Campagna, which Inness is so
fond of introducing in his Italian pictures. They give
an essentially foreign aspect to this locality. Across
the water, showing in faint purple outline against
the horizon, a beautiful mountain range melts into the
distance, while between skim white-sailed boats, or
dim, shadowy ships glide just indicated on the farthest
edge.   Coming nearer the house, one enters a grove
of live oaks and pines intermixed, bent by the fierce
northwesters into the wildest and most frenzied forms,
as if the dryads occupying them had been tortured
by remorse ; under these, winding paths run here and
there, bordered by emerald lawns which near the
house blossom into brilliant flower-beds of the most
magnificent and profuse kind.   In one place a cactus
garden shows every variety of these diabolical forms,
fascinating in their repulsiveness as the devil fishes so
many of them resemble, and gorgeous with a tropical
luxuriance of blossoms. A corps of forty gardeners
are busy winter and summer in this beautiful place,
and the results are worthy the labor devoted to it.
Some of the wild gardens, with hedges of foxgloves
ten feet high and every color of the rainbow, and
clusters of roses of such magnificence and regal amplitude, that they look hardly natural, make it seem as
if somewhere within those tangled bowers the sleep-

ing beauty might still be held in magic thrall, surrounded by her bewitched court. It would have to be
a very royal young prince indeed, who could ever
make up to her for breaking such a delicious slumber.

The house in the midst of this fairyland is worthy
the situation. A mass of towers and deliciously-
planned corners and angles, with broad piazzas and
shaded porches, it rises by terraces of steps from its
enchanted wilderness of flowers like another bit of
enchantment. It is beyond all cavil or comparison
the prettiest bit of architecture, and the most complete in its internal arrangement, we have seen in these
months of varied wandering. The service in the
dining-room is a miracle for swiftness and polite attention. We had grown so used to plate-hurling and
table-tossing, to waiting an hour for an order, to having cold dishes and uncalled-for dishes set clownishly
before us, and to taking them meekly, glad of anything from such imperious bunglers as the ordinary
hotel-waiters of the Western country, that it seemed
like reaching a haven of rest and peace to sit down
and have a well-bred attendant satisfy quietly and
quickly every wish of the heart. Even the Palace
Hotel, with its well-trained corps of assistants and
elaborate cuisine, cannot compete in anything but
waffles with this beloved inn. ' The Palace waffles are
things to dream of. Within its limited list of luxuries everything is well cooked, and sent to the table
as hot — well, as hot as hot — and that is one of the
first essentials for perfection. The Palace is of such
tremendous proportions that even if a waiter takes

your portion out of a fiery furnace, it has left all its glow behind before it reaches you. It is nobody's fault, and yet your innocent stomach suffers. Within easy distance, the most beautiful drives imaginable are to be found, and remarkably good horses and carriages to reach them. Groves, cliffs, beaches strewn with the great shells of the Abalone, lined with gleaming mother-of-pearl, Chinese fishing-villages with their picturesque collection of huts and people, ruined walls of adobe and quiet little half-Spanish villages, are within easy reach. The beautiful Santa Clara valley, fertile and fair, stretches away to the north, dotted with such pleasant towns as San Jose, Memlo Park and other pretty spots, while San Francisco itself is but three hours and a half away — for we are learning now to measure distance by minutes instead of miles.

I wish the dear people who are at the helm of our different eastern seaside resorts this summer would take a telegraphic trip here before the house closes, and carry back a mental inventory of luxuries for next season's campaign. The idea of Boston people being outdone by anything so Western as the Pacific coast, the very jumping-off place of creation! I won't ask them to take home the warm sea-water tanks under their crystal roofs, with the esplanade of waving palms and greenery throwing their soft quivering shadows on the bathers, for we have not the long Western purses which can afford to pay $75,000 for such a luxurious whim. But the glass-covered piazzas, where the sun makes summer even out of a winter day, with every rude wind shut out, and only sweet sights and sounds within reach of eyes and ears—*that* they might take; and the tiled fireplaces full of blazing logs; and the exquisite little rooms with their Turkish rugs, lovely enough to have come this moment out of Pray's window; and the parlor with its Steinway grand; and the garden protected by hedges and ramparts. Why cannot they make a Monterey by the Atlantic?

Returning to San Francisco, I must do the people the simple justice to say that our Eastern notions of their peculiarities are entirely and unwarrantably extravagant. The nouveaux riches at home have quite as much vulgarity and shoddiness and loudness, with a finical narrowness in the way of flaunting their pretensions in the face and eyes of the populace, which the larger-hearted and freer-handed Westerner never acquires. The few houses with which personally I had the pleasure of being familiar were exquisite in refinement and good taste, with a fine flavor of heartiness thrown in that is too often wanting in our more thin-blooded civilization. They were filled with a generous amplitude of comfort and luxury, both in furnishing and dimension, that our showy modern architecture would never admit.. They made many of us doubt whether even in building,

> "the reign of good Queen Anne
> Was culture's palmiest day."

From hallway to bath-room, from fireplace to frieze, there was a largeness as attractive as unusual. The young people who swarm through them, for there is

an old world sentiment in favor of large families which
does credit to the head and heart, were well-educated,
well-bred, and fascinating in that delicate fragrance of
modesty and unassuming simplicity which is to youth
what perfume is to the flower.   Within a few years
their home educational institutions have made immense strides.   There will soon be small need of
sending boys to Harvard or girls to New York board-
ing-schools.   I saw in the large halls of the college
of St. Ignatius, one of the finest sets of apparatus in
chemistry and physics I ever found in any place,
filling class-room after class-room with the best appli-
ances of modern art; and at the annual exhibition of
one of the private schools, we found a collection of
young girls, who, for talent, for sweetness, and for
perfect simplicity of dress and character, might have
borne away the palm from our darling ones at home.
The increasing tendency to display in our Boston
exhibitions has been a sore blow to many of us now
for years.   But how could any girl, with a girl's intui-
tive love for purity and refinement, be near the beloved
woman who is the soul of that San Francisco school,
and not become permeated for life with all good influences ?   One of the dearest wishes of my life would be
fulfilled if my little Happy-Heart could be near her.

It is a sincere pleasure to be able to take home this
remembrance of the city.   We have had for years
such a distorted picture of the social relations of the
place in our mind's eye, that this glimpse of its real
condition is comforting.   Not that there is not plenty
of room for improvement; any city as cosmopolitan

in its tendencies as this, must enclose an immense
mixture of good and evil. But the Eastern humani-
tarians who so zealously ignore the beam in their own
eyes, while pointing out the motes in the moral iris of
San Francisco, had better call on an oculist before
going any farther. It is a pity to spoil such a number
of the pretty little on-dits of polite society by doubting
their veracity; but I think the day is fast waning that
could give us stories of Mrs. Mackay and others of
her class desiring to buy the Arc de Triomphe. Even
without that reticence which comes with the habit of
riches, there is too good an understanding of their
own place and dignity to admit of such faux pas now;
and, as a simple matter of justice, I don't know why
we should pet our self-made men and women at home,
and sneer at them in San Francisco.

In a place of such magnificent proportions as this,
two weeks or three, is only an aggravation as a limit of
time. The Chinese quarter alone would occupy half
of it, in its bewildering novelty. A stranger's steps
turn as instinctively toward this queer precinct here,
as they would toward the Louvre at Paris. Perhaps, if I said toward Bon Marchè, it would be a
better simile, for candor compels me to admit that
there is quite as much enthusiasm expended on the
cheap bargains as the priceless pictures, by the majority of people who see "Yurrup." By the time you
have travelled with a detective through the by-ways,
you want to try the highways alone. The strange
little atoms of shops, with their clumsily-piled treasures of crapes, and carvings, and pottery, are like an

oriental bazaar. They look as if they held nothing;
and, lo! they contain all that heart can desire. The
most wonderful crapes, the most delicate embroideries,
the most delicious monsters in china and bronze, come
out, as if by magic, from the walls, the floor, or the
ceiling. China, bamboo, curios and fantastics, per-
fumes and paints, nothing seems impossible to get in
these dark little dens, if you are only ready to pay.
And *when* you have paid, then never lose sight of
your bundle until it is safe in your possession. They
have a habit of forgetfulness, an absent-minded way
of dropping two or three small articles out of your
purchases and letting it escape their recollection,
which is trying to one of business habits. But make
a note of the items, and don't let it elude your re-
tentive memory, and you can floor the almond-eyed
Celestial every time. And never give by any chance
more than two-thirds of the price first asked. The
more you succeed in shaving a Chinaman, the more
respect he has for your race; so you owe it to civilization to uphold its standard.

If you ever find yourself in one of the streets which
belong to this people, turn in at the first chop-house
you meet; climb one or two flights of stairs, until you
come to the uppermost rooms; choose a stool of
carved ebony from the pile at one side; sit down at a
small round table of polished teak wood and look
about you. There will probably be lanterns of a
gorgeousness you never before dreamed of hanging
from the roof, and screens and banners brilliant and
dazzling on the walls; there will be glass cases filled

with impossible figures, and glowing flowers here and
there; there will be a crowd of chattering Chinese,
some Mandarins with the precious red button on top
of the small silk cap, some immensely effective in
brocaded trousers of a richness that makes your un-
accustomed eyes weak, and some common people like
yourself. Take all this in, and then ask for tea. Ye
gods! such tea! such nectar as you will never know
again. They put a pinch of dry leaves into a tiny
cup; they pour boiling water in and cover with a little
saucer; in a moment they pour off this effusion into
still tinier cups like those of a child's tea-set; they
offer you sugar if you desire, but no milk, and every
few moments your copper-colored Ganymede comes
with a kettle of his own tint and pours on more water;
yet the last cup is better than the first. With it they
give you little decorated saucers of preserved ginger, of
baked almonds, of limes conserved in sugar, of fanciful
cakes made of nut-paste covered with brilliant frosting,
of strange-looking rice squares, and last, but not least,
a pair of chop-sticks, which, if you are a wise woman,
you will not try to tackle. The airy and easy way in
which your convives use them may deceive you, but
don't attempt to copy; be original, and let them
severely alone; and for all this dissipation you will
pay two bits, the value of which you probably know
by this time, but for fear that you don't, I will whisper
— twenty-five cents.

You will go to the Chinese theatre, of course, but
you will not stay there. Of all the grotesque, dis-
cordant, bombastic, infernal, inhuman tortures the

barbaric mind ever conceived, this is foremost. No
wonder an ordinary play lasts six months in the pre-
sentation, when between every word an actor speaks
there is a pause to allow the orchestra of three to
clash cymbals, and roll drums, and squeak a two-
stringed fiddle with a triangle hanging from it. The
orator wades through part of his sentence in this manner, swaggers behind the stage to rest, comes out at
the other side, takes up the broken thread of his
discourse, gets tired, goes in again, and so on, ad
nauseam. As among the ancient Greeks, women are
not allowed upon the stage, young men filling their
parts, with brilliantly-painted cheeks, gorgeously embroidered silken robes, and the most harrowing, unnatural, shrieking falsetto voices imaginable. As a
sort of protest of race, I suppose, men in the audi-
ence wore their hats, while every one in the women's
gallery went bareheaded, with hair dressed after the
fashion with which pictures have long made us familiar.
The hideously dreadful noise of brass and tin never
ceases, except for a second at a time, and the patient,
sad-eyed crowd, sitting quiet and motionless, filling
every inch of floor and gallery, look on with grave
satisfaction. There is no applause and no animation,
but an absorbed interest in what is going on, which
must be a comfort to the shrieking actors if the pandemonium about allows them to notice it. Ten minutes
were all our weak tympani could bear; but here the
motionless crowd sat for hours without any feeling
but delight. In spite of the most painful attention to
look and gesture, in order to get, if possible, an ink-

ling of the plot, we were obliged to give up in despair. Every sentence was delivered with the same terrific force and exaggeration of action, so that the declamation was one dead level of noise and fury.

The opium dens and gambling saloons we left alone. Seeing men make brutes or fools of themselves did not enter into our ideas of a holiday; but those who investigated thought them of interest. The water trips to Saucelito, San Rafael and San Quentin, gave us beautiful glimpses of what seemed the most beautiful harbor in the world. The water had always the same deep green color, that looked unreal to eyes accustomed to the blue Atlantic; the rounded, wooded islands and promontories made a succession of delightful views; the city climbing its terraced sandhills was always in sight as a bit of life, and the mountain ranges melting in the distance made the farther shore beautiful, with its white villages nestling in the shadow of the hills.

Then there were the Twin Peaks and the Cliff House, the Golden Gate Park and the Presidio, the Diamond Palace and the Shot Tower, the Fire Patrol and Ichi Ban. The cable roads themselves, are enough attraction for any one city. We saw them in Chicago, but without being at all impressed. To see a car and dummy going on a level plain· was so like common railroading that even the absence of steam failed to make it unusual. But here, where they go rushing up and tumbling down the frightfully steep sand-hills, which, like perpendicular terraces, surround the city on almost every side, they become one of the wonders of the world. A single lever-like handle projecting perpendicularly from the centre of an open car is the only visible machinery. A jerk to this side or that, propels two cars up the side of the steepest ascent, or stops it in the midst of an incline that leaves one almost in mid-air. I find copied in the Big Boy's diary a Chinaman's description of this motive power, which is so concisely vivid, that I copy it here, in spite of its slight Western flavor of profanity, which is as natural to this soil as its monstrous squash and gigantic beets, and almost as innocent: "No pushee! no pullee! go like hellee," was the gentle barbarian's formula, and it is the simple truth. It is very like witchcraft, and the unfortunate creature who invented it would have been burned at the stake by any respectable deacon in Salem, if he had only lived there two hundred or so years ago. But the times change, and we with them. Now we put money in our wise men's purses, and send them to Congress, when they achieve some new triumph of diabolical art. In spite of the cold, cold winds, in spite of the whirling sand and pelting fog, the outside seats on the dummy, which is not unlike our open car, are always full, even when the covered car behind is empty. There seems to be a fascination about them, though I can well believe what a medical man says, that consumption and lung diseases have increased largely since their advent. It would be too dangerous a pastime for dear Boston, even if it were feasible there. The infinite length of the business streets is crowded with shops of all kinds, not of quite such tremendous proportions as our representative Eastern houses assume, but of immense resources. In a small jewel shop on Montgomery street, we saw the proprietor showing a party some regal ornaments, a feather of diamonds for the hair, worth $14,000, and a close necklace at $40,000. One would imagine, from the lavish number of precious stones at each hand's turn on the street, that every one dabbles in stocks and puts his great profits into diamonds for his wife and daughter; for, of course, they all make great profits, or they would n't keep on dabbling.

If private and public report is to be believed, almost every one in the country, without regard to age, sex, or position, does more or less in the way of irregular stock-broking. The lady speculates with her pin-money; the servant, with her wages; the business man, with his income; the mechanic, with his hard-earned dollars; the bootblack, with the "bits" he makes on his "shines." The air is full of legends of the tremendous fortunes made by some chance turn of the wheel, now and again; a feverish anxiety to be in the lists, with the chance of some time or other bearing off a prize, possesses the community, and makes the market from which unprincipled men gather their harvest. The very uncertainty attending speculation becomes one of the elements of fascination, and only heightens the excitement of the chase. They bear disappointment as an Englishman bears defeat,— never know when they are beaten, and are ready to go into the struggle again, hammer and tongs, as soon as they recover breath. They may be "dead-broke,"

"cleaned-out," "busted"; but they are never too far
gone to stake their next dollar on the chance of
"striking it rich this time."   They are wonderful
people.   Other men would go mad over so many dis-
appointments, but the good Californian thrives on it.
They believe in "luck," as honestly as the Irish
believe in fairies; and, in the deepest depths of pecuniary difficulty, when the fair bubble which dazzled
them before has melted into thin air, they follow some
new chimera, certain that this time, at least, Fortune,
which has been "down" on them so long, will smile,
and crown them with her golden laurels.

CHAPTER XIII.

THE ECCENTRICITIES OF CALIFORNIA.

TO the stranger who enters the California about San Francisco, at this time of the year, it is a world of wonders; everything goes by contraries. One comes to the city to get cold, and goes to the country to get warm. The fields which are seen from the summits of the Twin Peaks, lying barren and bleak in the July sunshine, are clad in verdure and filled with lavish profusion of growth in midwinter. Farmers send their cattle to pasture in January, while they herd them in barns and feed on hay or grain in June. The usual sequences of life seem to be thoroughly upset, and one is constantly amazed at the series of surprises. Even on the vexed Chinese question there is an absolute opposition between fact and sentiment. Hatred of the Chinese is the one point on which all Californians, good, bad or indifferent, agree. There is no doubt or cavil in the Western mind when one asks an opinion in this regard. Absolute distrust or dislike colors all their dealings, and they speak with bitter scorn of the Eastern people, who, knowing nothing of the curse fastened upon them, still dare to talk and legislate in favor of its continuance. It is in vain to point out what inestimable help the Chinese have given, and are giving, in public works which white labor could never accomplish, in building railroads or canals, and in scores of other ways; that simply counts for nothing. They are looked upon with an aversion, compared with which all other antagonisms of race seem paltry. It is a war of religious prejudice as well as political difference. In the palmiest days of abolition tumult, the negro was never so wofully under the ban, as these helots of the far East are now on the western coast of America; yet, in spite of all this fury of scorn, in spite of this intense hatred which hardly stoops to reason with an inquirer, in spite of clamor and disaffection, they continue to employ the people they revile, and by so doing give them, day by day, stronger foothold in their towns and cities. They hold indignation meetings to prove that the Chinese laundrymen are driving out home labor ; that the Chinese kitchengardens have undermined an industry which in other states supports thousands of citizens and their families in prosperity; that the Chinese habits of overcrowding, and their phenomenal simplicity of diet, enable them to force all other laborers from the market by the infinitesimal amount upon which they can support life, — and there the matter ends. The very people who cry out most loudly, the very lower class who are being driven to the wall by this tremendous competition, employ Chinese washerwomen because they do their work for quarter the price; buy Chinese-raised vegetables because they can get them for a cent less in the pound ; purchase underclothes of Chinese peddlers, and tea at Chinese warehouses for the same short-sighted reason. Rich men rent houses to the authorities of the Six Companies, knowing that they are to be used in open disregard of law and order, crowded to repulsiveness, swarmed with humanity, until the number in each tenement is beyond belief. The law makes edicts to insure a certain amount of air and light to every adult within the city walls, and then closes its eyes, while twenty thousand Chinese live in quarters that would not shelter two thousand white people. The simple enforcement of the act regulating the number of cubic feet of air required for each person within the city, would drive three-quarters of the race to-morrow outside the limits of legislation. They could not begin to pay ordinary rates of rent, unless they charged ordinary rates for labor; and once they place themselves on an even footing in regard to expense, their doom is sealed. This namby-pamby trifling with a question concerning which they pretend such alarm, is not in keeping with the usual clear-headed, energetic action of Western people; it makes one suspect some hidden reason for tolerating a pet grievance for the sake of railing at it. *If* San Francisco really believes what it says about the danger of harboring this race, why do they not use the simple, legitimate means at their disposal? I cannot conceive Boston or New York, with a similar belief, tolerating any such internecine policy for a day; and I cannot conceive Californians in earnest in their cry of "the Chinese must go," when they take so little pains to protect themselves. To take all the Chinaman has to give, and then curse him for letting it be taken, is rather a superficial way of settling a difficulty.

In a city where people with one or two millions seem to be as common as those with as many hundred thousands in other corporations, and where local pride and affection run so high, it is a pity some large, generous, rational plan cannot be devised for irrigation, and properly carried out.   With plenty of water to lay the dust in the streets and cover the shifting sand-hills beyond with verdure, the first immense stride would be made in improvement.   With shade trees lining those beautiful wide avenues, and filling in the open corner spaces which come so often where three streets meet, San Francisco would be a joy to look at in summer time, just as all agree it is in winter.   If, in addition to this, the swift-climbing hills which rise from the water on every side were laid out in terraces, I think it would be one of the most beautiful cities in the new world.   The exquisite bay, with its islands and dusky background of foot-hills climbing and fading all around the horizon; the fine outline of Mt. Diablo, as it shows in the distance; the ever-present beauty of flowers adding its graciousness to out-door life, and the pleasant impression of comfort which so many pretty small houses make, interspersed with palatial larger ones, give all the requisites for great beauty. It has everything needful but water.   Out in the suburbs, the country is green as a garden, where windmills are employed extensively to irrigate from artesian wells or from ditches brought down from the mountains beyond.   I counted from the car-window, as we stopped for a moment one day at Valencia street, thirty-six of these enormous whirligigs turning slowly in the languid air, and giving a Dutch aspect to the whole country-side they were in, with its small houses and beautifully cared-for market gardens.

If we were older travellers, who could take the goods the gods provide, and never pause to think of any other; or, if we had come fresh from the inclemency of a New England winter, there would be more wonderment and more love for this golden land which puzzles while it pleases us. It would be like the beginning of new life. We would see only the beauty and such little stings as sharper air or an every-day fog-bank would be trifles beneath notice. But now one has all the memories of the loveliness at home to contend with. We know that balmy air and singing birds, daisies and buttercups, the universal freshness of youthful nature, are abroad on the hills and fields of June, so that the sharp atmosphere and clinging mist, the dust and imperfection here, is more than ever trying. Especially when in conservatories, one comes across, as we did yesterday, a handful of long, spindling, straggling daisies, set in a gorgeous flower-pot, tended with care, and looking delicate as things tended with care usually are, and one remembers the affluent fields of regal gold and white marguerites on the sunny slopes of Green Hill, is one struck with the inconsistencies of nature. All the luxury of wild lupin, in long spikes of blue and yellow, growing through the meadows, will never equal in beauty the wild rose hedges, the clover tops

and daisies, of the fragrant fields that lie beside the
Atlantic.

The climate of San Francisco is essentially its
own, however. Ten miles away in any direction, you
escape the direful, daily winds, the dust and discomfort. Cross the ferry to Oakland, sail down to
Saucelito or San Rafael, take the roads leading in any
direction toward the interior, and you reach shelter
before you are gone an hour. After ten miles, you
begin to feel warm; after twenty, you are in summer
again, especially if there be water near. On the way
to Sacramento, the river-bed widens into broad, shallow meadows, filled with cattle standing knee-deep in
the placid waters, and crossed now and then by flights
of birds, or made picturesque by tall white herons,
standing immovable amid the sedge, as if just out of a
Japanese picture. Sacramento itself, lying in the
midst of these moist green fields, may easily be, as
we understand it was, unhealthy; but at the same
time the abundance of shade and width of the fine,
regular streets, make it particularly refreshing to
look at. A pretty fashion is a wide upper balcony
built out from the second story of houses and stores,
shading the sidewalk below, and fringed with flowers
or trailing plants above. It gives a half foreign look
to a purely American town; so do the numberless
pretty small cottages, set in gardens, bright always
with bewildering flowers, roses eight inches across,
walls of white honeysuckle and stacks of oleanders.
I never saw in any other place such a variety of shade
trees as in this city. Locusts with long, fragrant,

drooping blossoms, elms, white oaks, pines, eucalyptus, even fig and orange-trees, were all to be found, over-arching the clean plank sidewalks; while in the gardens, our New England orchard trees, covered with bloom and fruit, brought a fragrance of home that made them still sweeter. We happened on a poor season to test the resources of the country in fruit, however. We listen to melting stories of the deliciousness of this or that dainty, to moving pictures of baskets full of toothsomeness for a quarter, that would cost a poor man's fortune at home, and we groan, tortured by unavailing longing; for we believe every word we hear. Some peculiarity of the climate makes one not only ready, but anxious to swallow the biggest statements. A kind of moral inflation takes possession of one. You may not see grapes as big as walnuts, in bunches as large as a camel's hump, but you know they are there, just as surely. Anything, everything is possible. Apricots were just beginning to come in, but were yet of poor quality; peaches were small and hard; apples only good for sauce; strawberries, from some peculiarity of weather, plentiful but sour, and wanting the delicious aroma of our native berry; it was too early for figs and pomegranates, and too late for oranges, so that only the always wonderful cherries answered our preconceived ideas of California fruit. The vegetables left nothing to be desired. It should be the paradise of poor men; for the climate does not require the use of much meat, and every form of succulent and delicious vegetable product literally overflows the markets and produce shops.

The Grahamites, and other sects that believe the eating of flesh harmful, ought to colonize Eldorado. They would certainly have every opportunity for practicing their pet precepts.

We found all things except fluids sold by the pound, which is a much more rational rule of measurement than quarts and pecks. One knows in this way the amount one is buying and paying for, which one certainly does not five times out of ten, by our dry measure. Who has not at some time or other of her life looked in awe and admiration at the amount of spinach or the number of large potatoes which go to make up a green-grocer's bushel? By weight, one gets an absolute quantity, while by measure one purchases different degrees of uncertainty, according to the state of the market.

We found, too, an utter ignorance of the small coins called cents, two cents, and nickels. A certain large-mindedness of the inhabitants gets into the eyes and prevents them from seeing anything smaller than a "bit" or ten cents. The rest they call "chicken feed." The newsboys offer you two papers for a bit, so as to overcome the degrading necessity of receiving five cents for one; the boot-black puts on his boss shine for a bit, except in some few low-toned quarters frequented by impecuniosity; the entire legion of sidewalk hucksters and perambulating showmen of striking bargains, put their wares upon the basis of a bit, and mount from that into the golden heights of the eagle. I am not sure whether bills are tabooed from some idea that the national banks are becoming insolvent, but we never saw a note during our stay in that wonderful country. All large change was paid in gold, and small in silver, which added weight to our pockets if it did nothing else. Perhaps that is why there are so many heavy men there.

On the whole we heartily liked San Francisco in spite of its dreadful climate. The generous amplitude of its dimensions, the generous kindness of its people, the immense strides it seems capable of making once its feet turn in the right direction, its barbaric gorgeousness of adornment, its superb contempt for small coin of any sort, the fascination of its "dummies" as they breathlessly whirl you up the outrageous little hills — all these and many other reasons force you to love it in spite of discomfort. If we had only come upon it in winter, how at once and forever we would have been its fascinated slaves like the many thousands of bewitched travellers it has won already. But they must take more care of their sewerage. There is too much typhoid malaria now for solid comfort. And after seeing what the lack of rain can do in that wonderfully endowed country, can it be possible that any of us will ever rail at the blessed summer storms at home again? May my right hand lose its cunning and may I be anathema, if spoiled pleasure or crumpled finery ever draw one word of lamentation or reproach from me, though the rain should flatten out my best Sunday hat half a dozen times in the course of this present season. For how much worse off we would be without it.

If every person leaving San Francisco for the East

is obliged to measure off the quantity of red tape we saw at the ticket office yesterday, in signing and coun- tersigning and witnessing, I wonder they do not give up the unequal contest in disgust. The one railroad which by right divine governs the Pacific coast seems to make the most of its prerogatives; but it is a ques- tion whether throwing so many barriers in the way of buying a passage is any material aid to business. Perhaps it is on that principle of human nature which makes perverse longing dwell most fondly on what is hardest to get. We never more fully appreciated the value of being excursionists, than when the little red book was handed over, signed, sealed, and delivered again, in a twinkling, and we walked off, free as air, while the herd of regular passengers stood, ruminant and glum, waiting each his slow turn. Fancy an Eastern populace waiting in that way for the privilege of being allowed to pay a railroad fare!

CHAPTER XIV.

AMONG THE MINES.

ONE who goes to California and returns without having seen anything of its mining interests, has lost unknowingly the key which solves many of the problems of society there. The romance, as well as the reality of the history of the State, is bound up in its gold mines. The discoveries which in '49 pushed the then almost unknown territory into a prominence unique in the annals of civilization, have been going on in greater or less degree ever since, so that the California of to-day throughout its whole extent is still honeycombed with those deposits of golden sand which made it the Pactolus of the world. We do not hear any longer of the wild fever of excitement which seized men in those earlier days, when home, friends, health and even life were thrown away like straws before the fair winds which were supposed to lead to fortune; a certain reticence that comes with years and experience, and a fixed method which takes the place of the old-time haphazard ways, have allowed a semi-obscurity to gather over what is still as active an interest there as manufactures are to New England, or wheat fields to Nebraska. The wild gambling of the stock exchange, with its insincere

manipulation of insecure property, is one thing, while
the earnest business which returns honest profits on
honest investments through the length and breadth of
the land, is another.   What we have been taught to
look upon as the most chimerical and rabid speculation into which fortune-seekers can enter, becomes,
west of the Rocky Mountains, the simple natural
business of the land.   Around it, in the small mining
camps, grow up the different industries which make a
people prosperous and a country powerful.   One never
realizes the power of gold so fully as here, in the land
which is its, by birthright.   Let but the yellow dust
show itself on hill, or plain, or wild mountain cañon,
in bare desert or fertile valley, and instantly from
solitude and silence the dead world wakes to excitement of life.   People gather, houses spring up, mills,
stores, schools, churches rise, as if called by a fairy
wand, and sun themselves in the light of prosperity.
By-and-by, when the supply of ore is exhausted, the
thriving settlement, like a body from which the soul
has departed, dissolves, and is gone almost as quickly
as it came, unless, meantime, it has developed other
resources.   The pick and shovel travel away in search
of other hidden treasure; only the devastated mountain-side and deserted "camp" remain to tell that
man ever dwelt there.

Nothing in the West is more sadly strange to
Eastern eyes than one of these ruined settlements.
It gives one a ghostly, unsettled feeling, to drive
through the village street, with its rows of closed
cottages on either hand, grass growing over the door-

steps, wild vines hiding the dim windows, and small
gardens overgrown with the sturdy weeds, which
fasten like squatters upon the lost heritage of industry. Here and there, a single inhabited house
makes the rest doubly desolate by contrast. An air
of mystery and desolation, which never belongs even
to the wildest or most remote regions where nature
alone holds sway, rests about these silent dwellings.
Something of peace and fitness goes forever from a
place which man has once used and then discarded,
and no length of time ever completely brings it back
again. The most isolated spot on which the eye can
rest, so long as it is left alone to the sweet influences
of the natural order, does not impress one with the
same sense of loneliness which a place once human-
ized and made conscious of man's presence retains
forever after. I remember one day, while driving
through a certain deserted village, noting one particular little cottage, built with more care than its silent
neighbors, that must some time have been a cozy home
for some small household. A porch, with a four-paned
window in each side, and a broad seat below them,
jutted out into a little garden, in which two tall clumps
of calla-lilies and a glowing bush of red geraniums
held their own yet against nettles and mountain
sorrell. On the threshold before the open door, two
tiny, brown lizards lay basking in the afternoon
warmth, the gleam in their bright jewel-like eyes alone
showing that they were alive. A long ray of sunshine
flickered across the floor and died within the open
fireplace in the chimney opposite, and the two small-

paned casements were covered with dusty curtains of cobwebs. Outside, amid a heap of useless remnants of household utensils, a rude wooden baby-carriage, broken and weather-stained, made the picture doubly pathetic. It seemed as if, indeed,

> " Life and thought had gone away
> Side by side,
> Leaving door and window wide ;
> — Careless tenants they ! "

It was as we rode into the foot-hills beyond the valley of the Sacramento, to see a little of the mining phase of California life while it was still at its best, and to visit one or two prosperous mines, in order that we might bring back some definite idea of what makes vital interest for so many, that we first saw these sad, neglected little camps. For sixty or eighty miles after leaving the city, the railroad passes through fields of wheat, stretching out of sight and covering the land at this season of the year with the lovely pale gold of ripened grain. Immense machines for reaping and threshing moved at intervals through the billowy, yellow expanse, so that one man accomplished the work of a dozen. Where steam was required, the wheat-straw, after winnowing, was used for fuel ; otherwise it was plowed into the earth again to act as a fertilizer for the next crop, or used instead of hay for fodder. The fruitful soil gives back two harvests in one year, always presuming that water is supplied, for dame nature is a thirsty queen even in this lavish country. Leaving the line of the railroad, we drove for six or eight miles, this being the width of the

fertile belt in the valley, through a repetition of these
harvest scenes, before beginning to ascend the foot-
hills ; then up a gradual rise through a rolling country
full of green glades and wooded hillsides, that was
more beautiful, so far as simple landscape loveliness
goes, than anything we had yet seen in California.
There was nothing of the grandeur or vastness which
made the road into the Yosemite wonderful; but
such deep dells, and fair, sloping meadows, such
curving heights and graceful back-ground of rounded
summits climbing into the clear, pale sky, such a
wealth of beautiful trees spreading grateful shade
over the hot road, and stretching in stately groves
far up to the horizon, we had not met before. We
made the journey in a private carriage behind a team
of the small but powerful horses which are so common here. I wonder no longer at the old grandees of
England, who used to make the tour of the European
continent after this delightful fashion. Next to walking, it gives the most lingering, loving look at the
beautiful world through which you pass, and one
exquisite scene merges into another by gentle gradations instead of the sudden whirling from post to
pillar of the railroad car. Given fair weather and a
pair of good horses, with a driver who knows what
he is about, and there is no such absolute luxury as
this mode of sight-seeing. But it would require a
Crœsus to be able to afford it, so we must wait for the
millenium before it comes to pass that we can indulge
in it. The winding road curved up hill and down
dale ; waving grain fields faded into the distance

behind, and spicy undergrowth of small pines and hemlocks crept nearer in the foreground. The brush was alive with quail, which ran across the road and into their haunts by dozens. Jack-rabbits scampered from their warrens, or sat with long ears quivering almost within reach of the whip-lash, if one could be wicked enough to use it. Now and again a small flock of the same dirty, draggled sheep we had met so often, (how wofully unpicturesque sheep are in real life) or a smaller flock still of the white, silky, long-haired goats, browsed on a pasture near the road, but there was no sign of house or human being. Once a group of Chinese teamsters, driving half-a-dozen market wagons, stopped us to inquire eagerly concerning a law which had been passed a day or two before, restricting the use of water in hydraulic mining. The long-contested battle between farmers and miners, as to control of water privileges, had just received fresh impetus from some judicial decision in favor of the former; and, as all the interests of this portion of the country depended upon the mines, there was naturally great excitement. "If the mines are n't allowed to run, you 'll all have to skip out, Johnnie, my boy," said our friend. "O yes! But mine gotta workee allee samee!" answered the practical heathen, with a shake of the head that set his long pigtail dangling like a drunken pendulum. It was no use to try to shake his faith in the future of the country.

Here, as elsewhere, the Chinese are hewers of wood and drawers of water. Whatever is too hard or too heavy for white men's bone and muscle, falls to the

lot of these helots of the west. Their patience, their
endurance, and their most frugal habits, enable them to
live and thrive where the most prudent pale-face would
starve miserably. They make vegetables grow in the
midst of barren plains; they wash riches out of the
refuse "tailings" of the gold flumes; they pit their
stolid capacity for labor against the brains and higher
intelligence of their employers, and always win their
point of making money. Every Chinaman who does
not die, or make so large a fortune that he becomes
imbued with the Americanism of wanting to make
more, returns to his own country, within a few years,
master of the five hundred dollars, which assures him
a competence for life. We met them in forty different
situations,—always busy, always smiling, and always
apparently content. It made us almost desire that we
might be allowed to tackle this extremely Eastern
question at home, to see the deftness, the swiftness,
and the astonishing capacity those engaged in house-
work showed. A little such healthy competition might
stimulate the jaded energies of our present household
brigade to real earnestness in fulfilling their duties.
At present, I believe no place in the world claiming
a high degree of civilization suffers more from the
tyranny or stupidity of untrained service, than the New
England states. To do the minimum of labor at the
maximum of price, seems to be of late years the
watchword of the order; and an honest pride in fur-
thering the best interests of the employer is one of the
lost arts in their kingdom. There are jewels among
them, to be sure, but jewels never come in mass; and

the ordinary house servant, one of the rank and file, in an ordinary family, is apt to cause nearly as much expenditure of moral force as she saves in physical exertion. The Chinamen have not been educated to this point yet. The instinct of centuries of submission makes them willing to work, so long as any work remains to be performed. Some peculiar race development renders them exact to minuteness in reproducing what has been shown or explained; and great personal neatness, which is one of the last things with which they are popularly credited, make them very valuable parts of domestic machinery, so far as material well-being is concerned. The moral aspect of the question I do not enter upon at all; it would need closer study and longer acquaintance to dare offer an opinion on that point.

But to return to the road through the foot-hills. The little mountain streams we passed were thick and muddy. Here and there a level place was covered with a smooth, shining deposit of yellowish clay. These were the "slickens" which farmers declare are ruining their prospects by destroying the fertilizing power of the water. The pure streams, after being brought in ditches and subjected to the uses of the miners, come down to them so impregnated with fine sand and debris, that they are useless for irrigation. It is to reach some fair settlement of this vexed question as to who owns the water that this long litigation has gone on from year to year, and seems to-day as far from final adjustment as ever. The only decision must be in some form of compromise. Either side has rights that can never be entirely set aside. Meantime each party goes its own way, irrespective of judge and jury.

The little mining camp we entered just at sunset, in the green hollow of the hills, with its one straggling street galloping down one steep side, and all the public-spirited buildings of the place hemming it closely in, was one of the prettiest villages we ever looked at. Even the rival grocery stores, each with its partisan groups of lounging miners enjoying their evening smoke, wore a look of interest to us. The roof of each broad piazza extended nearly across the road, and made unique porte-cocheres for the service of man and beast. The two little churches faced each other across the dusty street; the two hotels glared into each other's windows; the most home-like small cottages we had seen out of New England nestled in their bright gardens, half hidden behind vines of gigantic roses, or climbing honeysuckle, and screened by clumps of red and white oleanders as large as small trees. In one place the stream through the great ditch which furnished water-power for the mines, was carried under the road with a deep sound like a cataract; otherwise all was still. It was as different from the harsh idea our fancies had made of the baseness and blankness of a mining camp as can well be imagined, and we found the inner life of the houses as pleasant as their outer seeming. There were whorls of Japanese fans on the walls, and fluttering muslin curtains on the windows; there were pictures and easy-chairs and rugs; there were recent books and the Eastern

12

magazines, so that, except for the big summer kitchen, with its folding walls, which could make it at will either an open shed or a cozy room, there was nothing to remind one of the great continent between us and home.

The next few days among the mines were real experiences. One of the celebrated blue gravel banks, two hundred feet high, was being washed to powder by a gigantic stream of water directed at will against its surface by a pipe with nozzles ten inches in diameter, through which the stream tore with such fury and force that everything crumbled before it. Masses weighing tons were crumbled into atoms in this way, and swept down the long flumes and sluices, dropping, meantime, their precious burden of yellow dust to amalgamate with the quicksilver spread below. The water which did all this was brought in a continuous ditch, thirty-seven miles long, from its source in the lofty mountains of the upper country, sometimes bridged across ravines, sometimes tunnelled through hillsides, and watched along its entire length by a gang of overseers who patrolled its banks so many times every twenty-four hours.

At stated times the stream is turned off, the wooden flumes cleaned of their contents, the quicksilver evaporated in immense ovens and condensed again in retorts for future use, while the precious. sordid, blessed, wicked metal, the

"Gold, gold, gold, gold!
Bright and heavy, hard and cold,"

is run off into molds and sent off to be coined into that power which is able to do so much good —and so

little. At first our unused eyes found gold in everything that glittered; but we learned soon that the
real article had much less shimmer and shine about it.
It was not the first time, nor unfortunately the last,
that base metals have put on the false semblance of
preciousness and deceived ignorance, while real worth
remained undiscovered near by. But we soon trained
our perceptions and now, if you want judges of the
richness of blue gravel peppered all over with fine,
dull spots, which hold within them such a heritage of
power for good or evil, we are ready to be called
in as experts.

In this hydraulic mining, the men employed have
many advantages. They are in the free air and sunshine; the work is all above ground, where the fair
face of the world still smiles upon them. There is
something inspiring in this search after the treasure
which nature had hidden away so carefully in her
river-beds, washed down from the eternal mountains
thousands and thousands of years ago. One would
like to go at it one's self, and wrest from the bald,
towering cliff above. the secret hoard which makes
every foot of it precious. One would like to change
places for awhile with any of those great long-booted,
red-shirted fellows, hairy and brawny, who stand so
superbly in the midst of the roaring, rushing stream,
guiding its course and helping its work. It looks like
pleasant and healthful, if hard, labor, with nothing
dark or ugly about it, except the "slickens" which go
sweeping down to flood the bright meadows beyond.
We would like to have seen one of the blasts that

from time to time tear the perpendicular walls of the old river-bed asunder with a charge of thirty or fifty thousand pounds of gunpowder, so that the whole visible hillside quivers, as if in the throes of an earth-quake, and breaks in an avalanche of dust and broken fragments on the plain below.   Eye-witnesses of some such former events gave us graphic descriptions in the patois of the country of the fury and force, "the all-fired cussedness of the way the thing lit out." Losing such opportunities for sight-seeing is one of the unhallowed consequences of living, as we do, too close to sunrise.

But the quartz mining which we saw a day or two after, with its thunder of infernal machinery stamping and crushing the rock fed to it, with its fourteen hundred foot shaft leading men down to the bowels of the earth, to work, cramped for room, panting for air, one small candle only making a spot of light in the dreadful darkness, how different the toil for gold looked in this !   Even in the beginning, before it is yet refined or purified, before it has become the medium for buying, and selling, and bartering, and bargaining, how much hardship and suffering it causes already ! No wonder the Spartans made their criminals wear gems and gold, in order to dissuade honest people from love of the base, bright baubles.   Standing at the entrance to the dark chasm below, while the president explained how many millions in how many years had been paid out to complacent stockholders, one could only think of the inscription which Dante placed over the entrance to his Inferno.   No doubt if the superintendent and his regiment of subalterns could have read my musings, they would have laughed with scorn at the bare idea of any one being depressed, in the shaft-house of a flourishing gold mine, with plenty of ore in sight. But I would almost rather never know where the treasure came from; there's too much "bubble, bubble, toil and trouble," from the very commencement. It was a relief to hear that accidents are extremely rare, and that the men are perfectly satisfied with their work. They are well paid, able to live comfortably, and the life acquires in time a great fascination for them.

The amount of dividends paid in a quiet way by such mines as this, unknown to fame and the stockboard, owned by a few prosperous individuals, and only familiar to the region in which they are placed, is simply astonishing. This quartz mine, of which we have spoken last, is an example. Bought for a trifle in 1865 by eight or ten men, and worked ever since, it has missed but five times in paying a large *monthly* dividend on the original shares, while putting up at the same time stamp-mills, refining and leaching works, and giving employment directly to several hundred men. One can scarcely estimate the number they employ indirectly. A business that buys eighty thousand cords of wood yearly for private use, reaches out so far that it is hard to gather it all together.

On the way between these two successful mines, we passed many others, some moderately prosperous, some just "striking it;" others, alas! like the Luck of Roaring Camp, after the luck had left it, stranded and forsaken. But the pretty valley towns, full of bright, comfortable homes, with the general air of cheeriness which comes with prosperity, were sufficient guarantee that all the golden days were not yet over in California. Many of them, like that of Grass Valley, were particularly delightful spots for tired eyes to rest on. Nestled in the bosom of the ever-beautiful hills, the pointed roofs of its pretty cottages, only seen here and there, amid the wealth of embowering greenery, lavish in flowers and fragrance, with a sturdy backbone of thriving business streets, a whole staff of churches, a regiment of bright homes, and—thank heaven!—only a corporal's guard of liquor shops, it was charming enough to make one desire to stay in it. As a rule, in the west, the saloons outnumber all the other business places put together. We lunched at an unpretending hotel on the main street, which, for coolness, cleanliness and comfort, with its pretty inner court full of roses and climbing vines, made a most refreshing contrast to many more showy houses. It was kept by a Boston man, who had married a tidy Eastern woman; indeed, we begin to doubt whether there are any real westerners at all in this cosmopolitan country. Such towns as this are doubly welcome, after the sad, bare settlements of the Southwestern States, which made life look too hard to be borne by the average man or woman. The people, like all we have met in California, were exceedingly warm-heated, eager to offer any little kindness, even when we stopped only to ask a question. The dialect was peculiar, a little of Bret Harte, but not very much of him, mildly suggesting itself everywhere. They "allowed" that a certain man "lit out" from a certain place, and another "fit" a fire in the woods all night; and their slang was exceedingly piquant. But we did not come upon any chivalresque gambler, ready to kill a man and take off his hat to a woman at the same time, so that, on the whole, mining must have degenerated since Harte's time.

CHAPTER XV.

WE were most agreeably disappointed in the Nevada desert and alkali plains. After the unearthly desolation of the south, they wore a look more subdued than oppressive. At this time of the year, the delicate green of sage-brush, with the pale gray of the white sage, which covers so much of the territory, made a soft mass of neutral tint set in high relief by the dusky, far-away mountains, stretching on both sides across the entire country. The dazzling white of alkali fields showed itself here and there like hoar frost. Something of the delicious breadth and freedom which is found by the sea, moves one here also in the immense outlook which stretches away to the horizon. The Humboldt River played hide-and-seek through the valley along almost its entire length; now and again streaks or rifts of snow on some soaring summit gave picturesque effect to the entire range in sight, or frowning palisades straightly set in narrow gorges shut out for a little while the rest of the world. Little whirlwinds of fine dust were constantly rising, like inverted cones, and after keeping up a few moments of incessant whirling, blowing themselves into thin mist in the bright air. There was great grandeur in the vastness

and monotony of the scene, but nothing haunting or
depressing, as in the ghostly outlook of the southern
country; so that the day spent in crossing the desert,
to which we looked forward with such dread, was
really anything but tiresome; and the night before
reaching Utah, whether from some unexplained excellence of the sleeping-berths, or some unknown influence
of the beautiful brilliant atmosphere, which reminded
us so much of Colorado, was the very best and most
refreshing we had passed since leaving home. The
air, like that of Manitou, seems absolutely to scintil-
late with light and purity. One draws long breaths,
and inspires exhilaration. The stories of returning
miners, which have heretofore been regarded as absurd
western exaggerations, of refuse meat and offal drying
up, instead of putrifying or tainting, become easy
of belief. In spite of its barrenness, its lack of trees
and verdure, its surface of sand and rock, its dreadfully severe winters and uncomfortable summers, the
radiant atmosphere and glowing sky go far to compensate for all shortcomings. When we woke, next
day, at early morning, and saw in the light of the
dawning Sabbath the deep-blue of the great Salt Lake
sweeping toward the snowy Wahsatch mountains,
while the great, gray plain lay asleep in the shadow,
and the mountain tips were rosy with the flush of
coming dawn, it seemed for the moment like the
embodiment of rest and peace; yet, travellers who
have frequently crossed this waste, declare that at
other seasons the dreariness and dust of this part
of the route are intolerable. Our exceptional good

fortune brought us through without even a touch of ennui.

Perhaps because this unlooked-for pleasure in finding the desert attractive had made us expect too much, perhaps because unconsciously the blight in its moral atmosphere had chilled our physical perception, we did not find Salt Lake City as interesting as we anticipated. This was the more strange because the valley in which it lies is so exceedingly beautiful, enclosed within a framework of exquisitely outlined hills, with the deep, shining waters of the great lake on one side, and the green, smiling fields and waving trees of a fruitful country on the other side. It is like a lovely vision, a pastoral idyl, after the severe prose of the plains, which stretch beyond its mountain walls. Full of vivid color, rich in the promise of spring-time, eloquent of that peace and content which a beautiful landscape always breathes, it was a gracious sight, and unconsciously prepared one to be pleased with what came after. The small houses and farms had an air of great thrift and neatness, the herds and stock grazing here and there were unusually sleek and comfortable. In the city, the great width of streets, and their long lines of locust and poplar-trees, gave a certain stateliness to even the humblest locality, and the people as well as the children looked so comfortably cared-for that there was nothing to find fault with; but there was, even about their best institutions, as well as in the deportment of its population, such a glaring contempt for the beauties and amenities of life, that it grated on one after the first glance; the

well-being seemed so entirely temporal, and so far
apart from any corresponding spiritual perception.

The disdain in which they appear to hold preten-
tious dwellings and polite manners, was not the fine
feeling of those who know the greater value of higher
things, but the grosser instincts of carelessness in
those who have never yet reached even the best appreciation of lower ones. There is no truth in a
religion which tramples the purest and noblest instincts
of womanhood under foot; there can be no stability
in it. It is too dreadful a state of things for hope to
live through, or wretchedness to endure; and in spite
of my best desire to see the contrary, the faces of the
men and women about showed but differing repetitions
of the same unwholesome story. The few sensitive
ones looked unhappy; the many coarser, indifferent.
In all the sea of faces at service in the immense
tabernacle, these were the two prevailing types; only
a few were free from it, and these were either mothers
holding little babies, and happy in the care, or youths
of either sex too young to understand their abnormal
position. Even among the presiding elders there was
no subtle magnetism of devotion or refinement. The
poorest meeting-house of a New England village
would show among its deacons better heads and more
spiritual countenances than this stronghold of Mormonism could summon from the whole range of its
best class, to represent the hierarchy of its church.
The Latter-Day Saints, which is the title they claim
officially, show neither in face nor bearing the qualities
which we usually consider as belongings of those who

live in the odor of sanctity. There is neither calm
patience, sweet benignity, deep thought, soaring aspira-
tion, nor loving kindness, to be found in the looks
of these typical men. In their place, shrewdness,
obstinacy, and a complacent arrogance, strike the be-
holder with any but spiritual reflections—qualities
much more likely to be canonized by the Mammon of
Unrighteousness than the God of humility and peace.

The thought of the social ulcer which preys upon
society, embittered every practical aspect of this
country to us. It, and it alone, made the clear air
dim, the bright water running in the roadside ditches
muddy, the pleasant shadow of waving trees dark and
intolerable. The condition of things which allows it
to be possible in a presumably Christian country, to
point out the Amelia Palace as the residence of its
ruler's "favorite wife," explains its own weakness and
wickedness. The divine mandate which raises woman
to the sublime dignity of wife and mother has nothing
in common with such degrading comparisons.

Many of the clean, neat little houses (for the large,
Gentile fashion of taking up much ground for dwelling-
places seemed to have stopped outside the valley, and
the homes were all small and tidy), had the piazza
divided by a centre railing; and one wife and her
children sat on one side, while the other little group
occupied the other. Even where this outward sign of
division was omitted, we learned that some distinction
of place was made between the different members of
one family within the dwellings. It was customary,
or not unusual, to have one mistress and her depend-

ents in the city house. and another at the country
ranche, so that the master would meet some part of
his multiplied wife wherever he turned.   The one-
armed driver who took us through the town had two
wives and eighteen children.   One would think he
would need both arms for such a regiment; but he
seemed quite equal to the situation, and said with a
leer, which in Christian countries would not be con-
sidered consistent with matrimony, that he was "about
ready for number three now."   It was the ugliest
commentary we heard on "the institution," and by
a Mormon.

It looked peaceful and proper enough; but our un-
ruly imaginations put riot, and bitterness, and dreadful
thoughts enough in the souls behind those stolid,
heavy faces to make a moral tornado.   We tortured
ourselves more during those two or three days in this
stronghold of the Saints, as they call themselves, with
a defiant pride which looks gigantic by the side of
their assumed humility, than in all the hairbreadth
'scapes and positive dangers of the trip put together.
It was so impossible to connect those common-
place looking people and their commonplace ambitions
and works, with the hell-upon-earth which the reigning
condition of things would create in our own bosoms,
that it made us feel as if we were trying to reap the
whirlwind.   No doubt we did grevious injustice to
many a peaceful Gentile, by imagining him one of the
polygamous band, and hating him accordingly, while
we wasted yearning sympathy over this or that good,
honest woman, the one wife of her one husband,—for

Salt Lake City is no longer peopled by Mormons alone. A large and thriving portion of the population live their own lives and follow their own religion, without fear of avenging angel or thug-like Danite. Many of the prettiest houses in the best situations belong now to this colony, and the number increases day by day. So long, however, as the church co-operative system continues to exist, I cannot see that it leaves great scope for large business transactions outside.

As far as material prosperity goes, it requires very little time to become convinced that the political economy of the Saints is a success. Under the cloak of religion, the church follows its believers to the home, to the store, to the office, and retains a helping, as well as a grasping hand, in every affair of life. As a consequence, there is none of the squalor, none of the uncared-for distress, which is so harrowing in other cities. Every one looks well fed; every one is decently clothed; there is even a feeling of relief in escaping suddenly and completely from the velvet and diamond fever which seems to have prostrated every other womankind of the Western country. There is an honest simplicity which allows people to live in accordance with primitive rulings; they are not brought up against some rock of etiquette or conventionality at every turn of the rudder. There is a wholesome disregard of gloves and fashions; the cotton and woolen overskirts of six years ago, and even further back, sit cheek-by-jowl with the cotton and wool overskirts of the latest Harper's Bazar. Most of the

finery worn in the Tabernacle was as evidently of
home production as the Tabernacle itself, and no man
or woman seemed to feel the reproach or incongruity
of companionship with finer feathers. I say seemed;
for, in spite of the startlingly self-complacent and brilliantly ungrammatical report of a missionary brother
just returned from preaching the "new gospel of
faith" to the heathens of West Tennessee, we caught
many a furtive glance at the exceedingly modest
toggery of our own party, trying to detect whether
kilt-pleatings or box-plaits were most in favor with the
wicked world's people, or if we tied our pullbacks
quite as tightly as in eighteen hundred and eighty-one.
The mothers, sitting here and there through the con-
gregation, bared their breasts and nursed their infants
with most absolute unconcern of neighborhood; the
children, scattered broadcast through the immense
edifice, clattered through the aisles as if they were
sidewalks, dipped tin cups of water from the open
barrels just inside the Temple doors, laughed a little
and cried a good deal, after the manner of children
cooped up in a place of worship all the world over. -
When communion time came, there was little to
remind one of the sanctity of a religious ceremony in
the hastily broken bits of bread passed around in
plated baskets, and eaten with as much unconcern as
a peanut by every man, woman and child in the entire
edifice. I remember being very much impressed once
by a general love-feast of this kind in the Cathedral of
Notre Dame at Montreal; but there was not an atom
of reverence or devotion about the rite as adminis-

tered in the Mormon Church. The people, taken as
a whole, were the poorest representative body I ever
saw gathered; a heavy air of vulgar satisfaction in the
men and a weary unconcern, in spite of the simple life
and delightful atmosphere, in the women. In the
Temple, as in the street, one of the usual facts in
polygamy was further verified. The man of the house
sat or walked with the youngest wife, while the others
took post-graduate places. I remember one evening
walking a long distance behind a surly man, who was
beaming, as much as he could beam, on a rather
homely-dressed woman, while he threw back an occasional command to "get along," or "hurry up," to
an older person struggling with a cross three-year-old
boy, who walked submissively behind. They listened
in the church to the religious exercise with decorum,
but without the slightest particle of interest or evidence of interior spirit. It looked as if any one of
them might say, with Tennyson's North Country
Farmer listening to *his* preacher:—

"An I niver knawed whot a meän'd, but I thowt a ad summut to sáay,
    An I thowt a said whot a owt to 'a said an I comed awáay."

The classes from which, in the main, Mormonism
receives its recruits, would partly explain this lack of
animation or interest. Probably, no set of people in
the world are more material, or on a lower mental
plane, than the operatives of large English manufacturing towns, the miners of Wales, and the laborers
in small German farming villages. It is largely to
these overburdened lives, in which existence resolves

13

itself into a constant struggle to snatch food from the
jaws of want, that the preachers of this new religion
come with a gospel more of the body than the spirit;
with promise of lighter toil, better wages and increased comfort; with the vexed question of polygamy
left adroitly in the background for future discussion,
and only the broad, easy tenets of doctrine offered for
dull brains to ponder over. Unless report is more
than ever a liar, a majority of the "converts" to this
creed become aware of its most remarkable dogma,
after they are within the limits of Utah. Once there,
the wise laws regarding labor and expense, the system
of tithes, the patriarchal government, the amplitude of
ease which comes to almost every individual, half
hampers them by implied obligations, half blinds their
naturally obtuse religious sense, and makes them
ready to adopt any code which is laid down for their
observance. But it is no use to tell any woman, that
custom or prejudice, or even the uplifting of martyr-
dom, can make the sharing of her home rights and
her heart's longings, peaceful, or happy, or healthful,
for any other woman under the sun.

In spite of the pamphlets for sale in the lobby of
the hotel, which gave letter after letter from leading
wives and mothers of the kingdom, proclaiming their
entire satisfaction with, and approbation of, the peculiar tenets of their chosen religion, and the peace and
harmony in which they live with the three, five, or
seven other consorts of their beloved husbands, there
is a strong and invincible conviction that they are
speaking for a purpose. Their faces tell a truer story.

The well-to-do aspect of the city is enhanced by its beautiful situation. Every house, without exception, has its bit of ground laid out according to the owner's taste, so that instead of the inevitable tenement blocks in other cities, one walks here through streets lined with gardens and grateful with shade. The new buildings going up for religious purposes within the enclosure of the present Tabernacle, promise to be more imposing in style and finish than anything yet attempted in the city. Some few residences of the wealthier Gentile merchants, or the more prominent religious officials, are sufficiently elegant to be noticeable here, but hardly to make a show in other cities of the same proportions. The private houses belonging of old to Brigham Young, were remarkable for nothing but a certain aggressiveness of size, and had more the aspect of buildings connected with a community than with family life. We were a little amused on entering one of the recitation-rooms of the catechism-classes, to hear a body of small people repeating answers and texts in concert with more respect for the sound than the sense of their lessons. They were reciting the Sermon on the Mount, as we came in, going over and over again in unison each section, until it was learned by rote. That it was by rote, a lusty youngster just in front proved to his own satisfaction and ours by shouting out, each time, "Blessed are they that mourn, for they shall be comfortable;" while the teacher, unheeding, allowed him to shout away. It was the old contest between the letter and the spirit.

I wonder very much, that, with the clear streams

of water running at either side of their streets, the
people do not utilize part of it to moisten the intolerable dust, which is overpowering at certain seasons.
It shows a want of foresight not in keeping with such
practical tendencies. Every evening in summer a
train runs up the narrow-gauge road to several
watering-places on the road, and both Mormon and
Gentile avail themselves of the privilege of bathing
and seeing sunset on the lake. The evening we were
there was memorable for a glory of color that made
all previous memories of sunsets dim. Low on the
horizon, between a sapphire sea and sapphire sky, a
mass of gray clouds changed in a few instants to
flaming islands burning on an amber ocean; the terraced hills on the right changed their dull, sage-green
to a pale, luminous emerald; one solitary peak just
under the deeply-glowing sky wrapped itself from base
to summit, in a royal robe of purple; while across
the water, toward the east, the snowy points of the
Wahsatch Range caught a rosy flush from the reflected light behind them, as if the spirit of morning,
instead of evening, was spreading radiant pinions over
the world. There was the utmost incongruity between
this superb, yet harmonious, scene, and the crowd of
noisy bathers, full of rough fun, who bobbed, and
squirmed, and floated like corks on the densely salt
water. It was impossible to sink; one could sit as in
an arm-chair on the calm sea; there was no danger of
being drowned, but a fair certainty of being pickled,
so we wisely refrained from buying experience at such
a price.

The hotels of the city, though fairly comfortable, do not show the same care for the accommodation of guests as those to which we had been accustomed. One who was not there at the exact supper hour, had to wait the convenience of cook and waiter for even a cup of tea and a boiled egg. Any of the little luxuries of the bill of fare were utterly out of the question for late comers. We left in the early morning, so early that we had slops for tea, cold potatoes, cold eggs, and cold victuals generally. It was the worst meal we had on the trip, and the poorest service. Nothing was hot but our tempers : they were boiling. If their object was "to speed the parting guest," they succeeded admirably; we would not have waited longer for a kingdom. Besides, our faces were fairly turned eastward ; and once one gets on the home-stretch, after a long and changeful journey of this kind, all the blandishments of the stranger could not compensate for any added delay that would keep us from the dear hands already stretched in welcome. We were made glad, too, by a rain, a *real*, fine, down-pouring rain, acknowledged by the world, and welcomed as a blessed thing. For so long we had had no rain at all, or else had been obliged to smuggle it in under so many disguises, such as mist or fog, or some undefined quantity, as if it were a thing to be ashamed of, that we took genuine pride in the dripping, warm, delicious moisture: it was like the first breath of home. The beautiful valley, as we passed through it again on our way to Ogden, was lovelier than ever. It seemed as if, leaving the city, we left an incubus behind which had unconsciously been weighing upon us. Between the mountains on one hand, and the lake on the other, each instant brought a new point of loveliness to view; and one realized that here, as in the old hymn of our childhood,

" Every prospect pleases,
And only man is vile."

CHAPTER XVI.

THE fine scenery through Weber and Echo cañons lost something of its effect on us from the anti-climax of seeing it, after the more magnificent wildness of the Colorado gorges, just as the Nevada desert seemed tame after the fierce desolation of the Southern saharas. If considerations of climate and weather made it possible—as unfortunately they do not—to reverse the order of travel, and coming first, as is usual, across the northern route, to finish sight-seeing with the Denver and Rio Grande Railway, the natural progression of wonders would be better retained. A succession of the most admirable points of view are crowded on this small line, which, in connection with the Atchison, Topeka and Santa Fé, crosses and recrosses with a network of tracks the whole Southwestern country. It was a little odd to find ourselves in the native haunts of this latter road, which had been familiar to most of us before as the irrepressible acrobat of the stock-board, with a mania for bounding and tumbling, and find that it had a local habitation as well as a name. May its dividends never be less, for the sake of the sincere pleasure it gave us !

There is no portion of Western travel, however,

which does not possess its own special charm to one
who knows how to look for it.   We had heard the
great plains of Wyoming spoken of as decidedly uninteresting, but we found them quite the reverse.
There is great impressiveness about these immense
level reaches, covered with roving flocks and herds,
narrowed here and there by lowering buttes of bright,
red rock, or high-piled basaltic columns, but, for the
most part, vast, silent, and solitary.   Through all
these uninhabited plains, both north and south, full of
the strange majesty of desolation, the harmonies of
David's symphonic poem, "The Desert," which the
Boylston Club had given just before we left home,
rang in my ears like a solemn invocation.   The per-
sistence of the low C, which underlies the entire first
movement, and gives such solemnity to the composi-
tion, seemed particularly appropriate to express the
magnitude and isolation of these stupendous mono-
tones.   We rode in front of the engine thirty or forty
miles one day, through the brilliant atmosphere, which,
probably, belongs to every region of plateaux elevated
so high above sea level, until the swiftness of motion
and heavenly air produced an exhilaration never to be
forgotten.   Life may hold more inspiring moments, but
we are content for the present to rest here; although a
precarious seat on a cow-catcher seems to have as
little moral connection with inspiration as it would
be possible to bring about.   But mind does not any
longer depend on matter.   It was only in old days that
the muse required to pose on a pedestal; now she sits
in any easy-chair and uses a type-writer.

We were surprised at the invariably good meals which followed us through this route at such distances from any dépôt of supplies; and wherever, at any of the small stations along the line, an attempt had been made at irrigation, either by ditches bringing streams from the far-away mountains, or by means of wells, the lavish abundance of vegetation in flowers, trees and produce made the world beautiful for a little space, showing that both soil and climate were there, if only patience and prudence, like the rod of Moses, tapped and bade the living waters leap forth.

Fine specimens of quartz crystals, petrified wood and moss agates, were for sale at the wayside inns. At Green River, along with these, were a few wild animals, caged and lonesome, showing their dislike of being mewed·up in their rough dens, just as well as if they were part of Barnum's menagerie. It looked doubly unkind to see them captive in the very heart of this primitive nature, which was mother and nurse of all wild things. If it is a measure of safety to capture coyote and grizzly, well and good; but kill them kindly at once, and never let them beat their lives out in dull, brutish rage against the bars. It was at this same station that a very good specimen of Western humor, coarse but trenchant, was handed about in the shape of a set of rules and regulations belonging to the two-story wooden hotel at which we took supper. Quotations from it had been posted here and there in the offices of public-houses, even in the Valley; but this was the first time the entire document was forced on our attention. The office-

clerk is described in the bill as one who "has been
carefully selected to please everybody; can play draw-
poker, match worsted at the village store, shake for
drinks at any hour of the day or night, play billiards,
waltz, dance the German, make a fourth at euchre,
flirt with any young lady and not mind being cut dead
"when pa comes down," put forty people in the best
room of the house when the hotel is full, attend to the
enunciator, and answer questions in Greek, Choctaw,
Irish, or any other polite language at the same moment, without turning a hair." The evident enjoyment
with which this combination of Mercury and Ganymede distributed his caustic parody among our people
gave us a feeling that the sarcasm was meant to be
personal. Can it be possible that there are ever
persons from the East who make ridiculous demands
of Western innkeepers? I really wonder!

The forty or fifty miles of snow-sheds through which
the railroad passes during the first part of the home-
ward journey, are another novelty. Such constant,
unpremeditated plunges into obscurity, without rhyme
or reason to give warning of their approach, would
addle the brain of most people, but we are all so clear-
headed! Trains of emigrant wagons pass many times
a day, each with its troop of led horses, its populous
colony of little children, and escort of sunburned,
bearded men, looking with patient eyes to the still
farther west toward which they journey. I did not
realize before that so many settlers move themselves
and their belongings in this way, at this late date. It
looked pleasant and comfortable enough in the clear,

bright weather; but how the women and children must suffer in the wild storms which sometimes devastate this region! Flocks of antelopes were almost constantly in sight, bounding over the plains, not so graceful or pretty a creature as the tall, antlered deer we passed in going and coming from the Yo Semite, but still pleasant objects to look at.

It was somewhere here, on the way to Cheyenne, that we took on board an Indian scout, one of those who guided the government forces at the time of the Meeker excitement. We braved the lurid atmosphere of the smoking-car for a couple of hours one evening, in order to listen to the viva voce stories of this untutored hero. I am bound to confess that the real Indian scout is a very poor grub, when compared with the fine butterfly who takes his name sometimes in city shows. Your natural article is a plain, inoffensive-looking man enough, exhaling a strong flavor of tobacco, reticent of speech, a little awkward of manner, and dressed in the ready-made, ill-fitting suit of the poor man in all climates. There is very little fire in his eyes or voice; his hair is short, his beard unshaven, his gestures awkward, as if he needed the excitement of activity to make him self-forgetful. He gives you his plain, horrible facts in the simplest language, which is still more graphic than the stage eloquence of his rival; he does not call the Indians names; he hates them too much to waste words on them; he acknowledges they have been ill-treated, but agrees with every other Westerner that "they got to be stamped out." He is as unassuming and neutral-

tinted as any day-laborer, with not even a stray gleam
of the eye to tell you that over and over again he has
looked into the face of almost certain death, and never
left the shadow blanch his own. We were disappointed at first, as any women of taste would be,
remembering the splendid chevelure and flowing moustache of Buffalo Bill and Texas Jack, the defiant
swagger of the fine animals, their broad-sashed waists
and fringed leggings, their wide Gainsboro' sombreros
and brilliancy of blanket and daring. The memory of
those stately heroes, riding arms akimbo, and eyes in
a fine frenzy rolling, up and down the city streets, at
the head of their war-painted braves, was still fresh in
our mind, and put the modest nearer view out of
focus. To see one such creature as that was balm
to the spirit; you felt that " One blast upon his bugle-
horn was worth ten thousand men," and that, somehow
or other, the small, quiet, modest fellow before you
had cheated you of something; but, like a woman of
taste, also, you changed your mind before you had
talked an hour, and believed that if there was any
cheating it was on the other side of the house.

We could hardly be sufficiently grateful for the
weather which followed us, making every day a new
benison. At the dinner-station they told us of a hail-
storm a week ago, which broke every window on one
side of the train, and at Cheyenne we found that a
rain-spout yesterday —which is the same storm as
the "cloud-burst" of Nevada—nearly devastated the
country. Between and among perils of many kinds
our large party skim or glide with only the best of

good fortunes, and day after day gives us a new reason
to be thankful.

One could almost tell when the boundary lines are
passed by the great change in the outlook in different
territories. Gray sage-brush in narrow valleys or
wide plains in Nevada, the mountains far away and
dark, with the same dusty look as in New Mexico, but
sometimes closing suddenly in abrupt palisades, like
those of the Hudson river, only of more decided
basaltic formation. In Utah, the ranges drawn together in narrow cañons of great beauty; in Wyoming,
the vast extent of high table lands, seven or eight
thousand feet above sea level, a natural grazing ground
for numberless cattle. What subtle madness causes
a stampede among these creatures and forces them
to cross the track before an advancing train, nobody
knows. But the whistle shrills constantly to warn
them, and then the engine slows to avoid running over
the stupid creatures, who won't be warned. I am
disgusted with cows. Their methods are too feminine,
especially when it comes to crossings. Have not I
seen the same unaccountable hesitancy, the same spas-
modic jerkiness of approach and retreat, and finally,
the same wild rush in the very jaws of destruction in
the civilized streets of my native city? Alas! have I
not done it myself? And how hard it is to see one of
the pet weaknesses of your sex emphasized by a four-
footed bungler of the same persuasion. The mountains seem to grow lower as we reach our highest
grade, and shortly after passing Sherman they disappear entirely, as the road goes down the opposite

slope of the Rockies toward the beautiful grain fields
of Nebraska. These are like Kansas, without the
hedges which made such 'noticeably lovely divisions,
without, also, the large, comfortable farm-houses which
have been replaced in all our journeyings since by the
poor, bare shanties of new settlements. The appearance of a desperately barren social life which these
little settlements present is depressing even in the
midst of the beautiful world surrounding them. There
was some kind of harmony between their blankness
and the desert places in which they were set in other
localities, but here the bleak, harsh look forces itself
to the front. There is also a noticeable lack of
wild flowers, after the lavish beauty of the south in
this respect.

The situation of Omaha and Council Bluffs, twin
cities on opposite sides of the Missouri, is delightful. Broad, green meadows, surpassingly fresh and
brilliant, stretch up to bold cliffs on one side and tree-
crowned hills on the other. Nestling in the rich foliage
which lovingly overshadow them, the pretty, prosperous homes of the young towns put on an attractive-
ness Western homes too often want. Nothing can
be more meagre and cheerless than these, as a rule.
One can easily believe their occupants comfortable,
but not so easily happy. The aspect of content or
cheerfulness which flowers and shade add to the house
they surround is almost entirely absent. It would be
an insult to the perceptions of the Western people to
doubt that the fault will be remedied, when means
of irrigation become more easily available. Here at

Omaha, as indeed largely through the whole of Nebraska, nature has done everything for her children.
The luxuriant trees could not be more beautiful amid
the palaces of kings than around these homes of the
people. The great, muddy, whirling river, which
divides the cities, with its uprooted snags, and broken
trees sticking in its shallows, hardly impresses one as
being capable of such magnificent outbursts of rage,
as sometimes seize it at earlier and later seasons ; and
it is with real incredulity we hear of last year's uprising, when it filled a space four miles wide with
rushing waters. Like Thomas of old, it requires that
we should be shown the places where the wounds
were before we believed ; then we understood, as never
before, what spring floods must mean to the inhabitants of river countries.

Iowa is a relief; still more beautiful than Kansas,
more undulation, more trees, more exquisite cultivation; frequent towns, and between them, for days,
hardly an inch of unreclaimed land; the cottages
improving in the look of thrift and industry, and an
ease of surrounding which speaks of a life less harshly
devoted to the hard grind of labor.

Rock Island is another lovely spot, as it rises like
an emerald set in moonstones from the gray shining
of the Mississippi, which sweeps grandly by just at
this point. Illinois does not entirely carry out the
promise of Iowa in cultivation; the farms toward the
east, though broad and green, show less evidence of
care. But clover fields begin to appear, the dear,
homely red blossoms which we have not seen before

this year, except for one tiny patch in Salt Lake
Valley. How honest and good it looks! Towns and
villages come thick and fast now, and here and there
broad fields, with furrows miles long, stretching away
like the strings of some enormous harp. The cattle
stand knee-deep in shining pools, and little rivers
begin to cross the track. The color of the green
through this entire state is superb; it is at once delicate and brilliant to a degree we never knew before.

Indiana, Ohio, Pennsylvania, each runs up the gamut
of delightsomeness, as we speed through it with the
dear refrain of "Home, home!" beating time to every
turn of the wheels bearing us on. The water, which
has been so terribly off color, clears itself from even a
taint of suspicion; the beloved, familiar wild flowers,
buttercup and daisy, wild rose and convolvulus,
chickory and yarrow, creep into fields and hedges.
We forgive even the ugly Virginia rail-fence where it
wobbles across lots, and the immense distance behind us so foreshortens the bit of travel yet to come,
that when we change cars at Buffalo to run up to
Niagara Falls for a short time, it seems like an afternoon frolic, and that we will be at home for tea.
After nine thousand miles, who is going to count two
or three hundred? Yet I have known the day when a
trip to New York looked of such magnitude, that it
took my mind a fortnight to prepare to grasp it, and
no doubt the same time will come again; for, as the
deacon said to Widow Bedott, "we are all sech poor
critters!"

CHAPTER XVII.

A GLIMPSE AT NIAGARA.

IT is always experimental to test a youthful memory, by bringing it face to face with the same scene twenty years after. The sorcery of time is no black art: it softens harsh experiences and brightens dull; it throws more light upon sunny spots, and deepens obscurity over dark ones, until at last they fade from sight altogether, and only happiness is left in bold relief. It was this consciousness that threw a chill over the thought of seeing Niagara again; Niagara, the one glowing picture of the outer world, which had crossed the horizon of a young girl's home-life to remain for nearly a score of years its highest ideal of beauty and grandeur. It is hard to have an old love made light of, even to increase the glory of a new; if the surpassing wonderments of the last two months should overshadow this, and make it hereafter take only a second place, how would my steadfast mind ever accustom itself to the change?

This was the dread which exercised me during the short ride from Buffalo to Suspension Bridge; this was the dread which floated away with the first glance at the rushing river; for is not "a thing of beauty a joy forever?" Was there not the old enthusiasm, the old delight, waiting to snare us in whirling rapids.

in majestic fall, in the wild commotion of whirlpools
below? Was there not the same wonderful green,
like no other bit of color in the wide world, in the
curve of the horse-shoe; the same sublimely direct
force in the straight plunge of the American side?
The little quaking tower was gone from its perilous
position on the upper edge of the cataract; but the
deeply-fretted tumult of waters about the Three Sisters and the lovely shores of Goat Island, was still
the same. Surging mountains of spray, rising like a
soul after resurrection from the abyssmal leap of the
river; symphonies of sound and color in the deep
thunder of its roar, the changing emerald of its waters;
there they were, all and more than all my fancy painted
them. Aye, even to make the illusion perfect and
cause my sober pulses to beat with the fervid rage of
twenty years syne, was there not the same irrepressible
hackman, bullying of manner, monstrous of charge, a
Shylock as of old in search of shekels, and ready as
ever for his pound of flesh? Even the ægis spread
about us by Raymond's coupons, which had carried
us victoriously through the battle-fields of monop-
olists in so many campaigns, was useless here. One
man bullied us first and abused us afterward; but I
am proud to record that we were proof against both,
and that he did n't make enough out of us to buy salt
for his porridge — if the wretch ever eats any.

The policy of building another suspension bridge
near the falls, at the same great height as the old one,
and making it wide enough for only one carriage at a
time to pass, so that the line desiring to go must wait

for the opposing line to come across, at the expense
of much time and temper, seemed very strange to us.
Possibly, like most international policies, it was neces-
sarily conservative, and conservatism is always narrow.
American enterprise at both ends of the line would
never have tolerated such halting movement. American enterprise would have done well to curb its vault-
ing spirit, however, before it builded those warehouses
and used the falls for water-power, to help its worship
of the almighty dollar. We could easily have borne
a little more conservatism there. One can understand
the action of Ruskin and his followers in petitioning
Parliament to refuse a charter for railroads through
the English lake region, when brought face to face
with the sacrilege here. For there are certain spots
that, by reason of reverent association or divine right
of majestic beauty, should be set apart forever from
the insolence of commonplace association. But there
will always be a class ready to oppose this feeling
as sentimental — to put a lager beer saloon in Shaks-
peare's house, a toll-gate and turnpike on the way to
Mont Blanc, and a concert hall in the vestibule of
Saint Peter's, by way of working pecuniary profit
from the hold these places possess over the imagination of susceptible people.

It is easier to go sight-seeing now at Niagara than
it used to be. Queer double-barrelled inclined planes,
which shoot cars up and down from the river bed,
take the place of the old steep scramble over the precipitous walls of the bank. It did not seem quite
such fun as the other, but it left you with more breath

and less flurry to revel in that glorious fury of waters
which lashes itself into foam and passion within its
pent-up channel.　There was greater fascination in
watching this wonderful tangle of malachite, where
green ran through all the shades from white to black,
than in looking at the calmer grandeur of the majestic
falls themselves farther up.　There was something
more in accord with the petulance of human passion
about one, while the terrible calmness of Divine rage
sobered the other.　We had a matchless day in which
to see this other wonder of the world — a sky and
atmosphere that might have been taken from Colorado
for depth and purity.　It appeared to me still that the
Clifton House, on the Canadian side, had much the
advantage in situation, and an appearance of retire-
ment more in harmony with the awful beauty of the
scene before it.　If one could have a little more time
for that deliberation and rest, which ought to be part
of the delight in any such place as this, it would certainly be here that one would choose to spend it.　The
world ought not to push too near the gates of any
such paradise.　This is what makes the bustle of the
little American town distasteful, with its petty traffic,
its hurry, its busy streets and modern houses.　There
is something sacrilegious in going out of the back
door and into the byways, as it were, to look at what
is really the life-spring of the place.　On the British
side you are brought first, and as a matter of course,
face to face with its chiefest glory.　But in the American quarter it is on the piazza which fronts the village
street that the guests sit to watch omnibuses from

incoming trains, to ogle village beauties, to note the modest business going on in village stores. There is nothing to tell that you are within a thousand miles of the great cataract, the echo of whose name fills the world. One cannot but feel that the isolation of the Yosemite ought to be here also, the reverent approach which prepares the soul to be in tune with its surroundings. Pilgrim schoon and scallop shell, which were signs of old of the true believer on his way to the shrine of his devotion, have given way now to express trains and fast boats advertised to make the through trip in a certain number of hours. We must make our pilgrimages in a hurry, or we can't make them at all. I am not sure, however, that we do not lose something of more value than even time and money in the bustle. To rush as fast as steam will carry you into the heart of the stronghold, to rattle up to the front door of the International and out of the back door, with only the narrow limit of Goat Island as a gateway, before you are precipitated into the holy of holies, this is not in keeping with eternal fitness. I am beginning to think they do things better in the West, where you must pay for your whistle — and how much paying has to do with appreciation! But it must be that constant motion has clouded a usually clear head; after the agony we suffered getting into that Valley of Paradise in California, am I actually grumbling at reaching Heaven too easily here? And growling over vulgar traffic and village stores, when we bought thereby spar ornaments

and Indian bead work, to add to Santa Fé filigree
and Pueblo pottery in the already over-full trunks ?
Surely, " Frailty, thy name is woman."

Sunset on Lake Erie was another picture of glowing
beauty to hang on the walls of memory; the ruddy
glow of the western sky and the path of flame it made
across the water would have delighted the soul of
Turner, but no other man would ever have dared
handle it. A cloud of myriads of gnats or midges,
which followed us from Suspension Bridge back to
Buffalo, somewhat obscured its radiance at the time.
How large a pleasure the sting of an atom of volatile
mischief such as this can spoil for one !

We woke the next morning — the last morning —
near Albany, in a scene of such exquisite pastoral
loveliness as one can only get by the Hudson on a
June morning. The low, rounded hills were covered
with trees and verdure ; the meadows were fresh
as an English lawn ; the beautiful bright water of
the brooks and creeks sparkling and flashing in the
sunshine, made the memory of the muddy Western
streams like a bad nightmare. What ease and comfort about the pretty houses ; what home-like thrift
about the small farms ; what nestling peace surrounding the church-crowned villages. Ah ! let them say
what they will about the newer world toward the
setting sun ! There is more room there, and chance
for prosperity, more material for brawn and muscle,
more money-making and hoarding up of riches, broader
lands and softer climates ; but here, here in New York

and Massachusetts, is the place, after all, for the white man to live in. " For is the life not more than food, and the body more than raiment."

What matters the smaller purse, if the happier spirit goes with it? And, in all honesty, I must declare, that, except for the very poor, whom life pinches in these crowded eastern settlements, life is an easier problem here than amid the bare, laborious experiences of the farther country. Toil is too solely the arbiter of destiny there; help of congenial companionship, little aids to educating the mind and elevating the spirit, the thousand nameless and unnoted charms which an older civilization spreads so lavishly about us, that we only heed when we are deprived of them, even the small conveniences which have become so much a matter of course with us, that we take them as we do the free air of heaven, without recognition or gratitude; all these are things to be dreamed of and longed for, but not possessed.

I fancy that life in those Western wilds must press more hardly on the woman than the man. It is always so where the rudeness of nature still holds the upper hand. A man's mind is taken up with many projects; he is out in the free air under the beautiful sky; the rougher experience which comes to him rouses a manly strength of antagonism which is part of every honest character; there are novel and exciting happenings every day; but a woman's horizon is usually bounded by her immediate surroundings, and where there is little to enlarge or enliven this, she is apt to sink into that condition of apathetic dejection which marks the bondage of labor everywhere. The towns and cities are of course very much better off; yet I think that if people generally made up their minds to live in the east, as they are obliged to in the west, to dwell in simple houses, eat coarse food, forego mental training, social advantages, personal comfort, amusements and society, there would not be a tithe of the difference there is now in the yearly account of profit and loss.

Even luxury in those distant territories cannot attain the enjoyments, temporal and spiritual, which are as much parts of our usual moderate life here as sunlight. (That is a bad simile; there is n't much sunlight left in to spoil the carpets of our comfortable New England homes; I should have chosen some other universal but despised gift of God.)

In climate even I am inclined to think we have the best of it. For delicate people, in whom great changes of temperature produce gradations in healthfulness, there can be no question as to the propriety of going where the world swings always between two or three degrees, and the equal air keeps the even tenor of its way through all seasons. But for persons born without special ailment, I cannot help feeling that the wide range of countries which know both winter and summer is healthiest as well as happiest. There are virtues of mind and body, notably those of vigor and endurance, which seem to require the struggle with cold or inclemency to develop. Any one who has

ever felt the invigorating heartiness of a walk on a
cold day, and the strength with which brain, as well
as body, works under the fine inspiration of a keen,
clear atmosphere, knows that the more seductive
sweetness of summer never brings an equal incentive.
The climate which offers the recurrence of these
differing experiences ought to be richer far in material
for nerve, muscle and brain, than that which is confined within narrower limits. Even home affections
grow stronger when they are nursed by the fireside.
It would be unfair to judge East and West by the
same standard to-day : both advantage and disadvantage are too unequally balanced; but whenever the
time comes to make comparison possible, I am ready
to prophesy that the more changeful seasons will have
the highest place.

It was worth going away from home if we brought
back nothing else than this content with the dear old
spot to which we belonged; and coming through
western Massachusetts through that long June day,
fresh from the delights of the shining world beyond,
which we had enjoyed so thoroughly, we realized with
new delight, as the swift miles flew past, that for
human nature's best development, there was nothing
wanting in the country about us. Back came the
beloved daisies, foaming in white billows across green
meadows, and the fragrance of dull, red clover ; back
the dear rock-ribbed fields, with their mellow toning
of sorrel in brown and terra-cotta; back the precise
little market-gardens and the thriving towns which

made them profitable. Even the mills and manufac-
tories looked as if the corporations who built them
had some apology for a soul, as the lines of clean,
little houses crept up under the shelter of the one big
building, like a brood of chickens under the wing of a
mother hen. How palatial they looked after the one
or two-room board-shanty, opening directly from the
gray desert of the plains! And the comparative moral
cleanliness in the lessening quota of saloons and
drinking-dens, if smaller material number is any indi-
cation, numerous enough, heaven knows! yet, but
not with the infernal preponderance of Western custom, where it looked as if every half-dozen men must
own a private bar-room. I know that many intelligent
people stoutly deny that there is any greater proportion of intemperance beyond the Rockies than here
at home, and so far as cases of actual drunkeness go,
they may be able to uphold the statement by genuine
statistics. But that does not change the absolute
fact of the universality of the custom of drinking.
A thousand ingenious reasons are offered for this:
the difficulty of procuring good water, the peculiarities of climate, the life of greater hardship and
exposure, the heterogeneous conditions of society,
and even the large-hearted generosity of a people
who like to show their friendliness in even such
small matters as "setting up drinks for the crowd."
No doubt all these have weight, yet none of them
make good excuse for an improper and dangerous
custom.

And now, as the afternoon sun drops lower, what fair city is this that rises in the east, throned like a queen above the silver Charles, many-towered and pinnacled, with clustering roof and taper spire? How proud she looks, yet modest, as one too sure of her innate nobility to need adventitious aid to impress others. Look at the æsthetic simplicity of her pose on the single hill, which is all the mistaken kindness of her children has left of the three mountains which were her birthright. Behold the stately avenues that stretch by bridge and road, radiating her lavish favors in every direction; look at the spreading suburbs that crowd beyond her gates, more beautiful than the parks and pleasure-grounds of her less favored sisters. See where she sits, small but precious, her pretty feet in the blue waters that love to dally about them; her pretty head, in its brave gilt cap, as near the clouds as she can manage to get it; her arms full of whatever is rarest and dearest and best. For does n't she hold the "Autocrat of the Breakfast Table" and Bunker Hill, Faneuil Hall and Harvard College? Do not the fiery eloquence of Phillips, the songs of Longfellow, the philosophy of Fisk, the glory of the Great Organ, and the native lair of culture, belong with her? Ah! why should we not "tell truth and shame the devil"—does n't she bring to us the babies and the family doctor?

To the portion of the pleasant company who have made the long journey together—for some still hold their heads to other stars and some yet linger by the way — I would rather say au revoir than adieu, wishing to each of them, meantime, "gluck auf," in the formula of another good-natured wanderer, "Here 's to your good health and your families !   May you live long and prosper."   I reserve for another chapter what I desire to say on the general subject of excursions.

CHAPTER XVIII.

PROS AND CONS ON THE SUBJECT OF EXCURSIONS.

IT is a significant though much neglected fact, that both the Greeks and Romans made their spirit of wisdom a goddess. Astute as they were, they understood thoroughly that no masculine divinity could have possessed the staying power of holding back trom conclusions before all his premises were before him. Only a woman could have the clear eyes to see the truth where it was hidden, and the clear head to retard her judgment until she had unearthed the whole of it. If this theory disagrees with later opinion on the subject, it would not surprise me; men have had too much to do with the world of late years to get a fair show for woman without a fight for it. But I would simply like to point them to the truth that it was Pallas Athena who sprang from the brain of Jove, a full-statured, well-armored, solid, intellectual fact, and the Greeks knew what they were about when they worshipped her. This is why, out of loyalty to my sex and an idea, I have waited to the end before hazarding any incomplete conclusions; a rash, misguided man, spoiled by a long course of political bias for ever being able to look judicially at anything, would have swamped you with contradictory opinions a dozen times in the record of these three months.

I confess to having had a strong bias against excursions in the outset. The disadvantages of such modes of travelling are apparent on the outside. There is the planning of a trip by some person or persons unknown, whereby your time is absolutely disposed of, and no chance allowed for exercising your own predilections as to hurry or loitering. You are wound up, so to speak, at the start, to go for a certain number of days or weeks or months ; you know beforehand where you will turn up at a certain hour, just as well as you know the ultimate end of the letter you put in the post-office. Besides, you are one of a crowd ; you are not an individual, endowed, as the catechism hath it, "with understanding and free will," but an atom, to be pushed or hindered in common with the mass to which you belong. This to a sensitive nature, counts for a great deal ; for though personality is in a measure lost, there is a publicity given to all one's movements, which has the effect of making one feel notorious, and notoriety even of a pleasant kind is distasteful to many. You feel labeled and ticketed like your trunk and shawl; or you feel as if you were going to feel so, which amounts to the same thing so far as you are concerned.

But here the drawbacks end ; and the advantages, which overbalance them a hundred fold, but which, being weightier, do not rise so easily to the surface, begin to claim recognition. By becoming one of a Raymond excursion party—for I will speak only of what I know—you are enabled to start on your pleasure jaunt with the first grand requisite for true enjoyment: a mind absolutely free from care about your destination or your belongings. Your special section of your special car is always ready for you; no matter how roads change or trains are made up; you hold the same relative position to the end, and see the same friendly faces near. This gives a home feeling that no haphazard arrangement of neighbors could offer, and makes itself felt as a real boon before the devious journey is well begun. You have no thought of the morrow; wiser heads than yours are arranging your rooms at the next stopping-place, seeing to the transfer of your luggage, planning your rides and drives with congenial company, so that when you enter the carriage and drive to your hotel you find your own trunk in your own apartment, as if it had grown there. Any one who has ever experienced the delays and annoyances of even an ordinary journey in a new direction, by reason of hackmen and checks, hotel porters and clerks, will appreciate what this means. The long route of travel is subdivided into a succession of short trips, with a few days or nights' rest between each; in every new city, prominent points of interest are grouped together and brought to your notice; whatever is worth seeing is thrown open to you without any of the usual formalities of introduction; you are lodged always at the best houses; and, although it is impossible for every one in so large a number to have the very best room on the very best floor of each house, you will find your accommodation quite as good as the average. It is often very much above this; for, whereas, when alone, some sudden

influx of travel may so fill your chosen hotel as to leave
for you only a closet or a cot-bed, as one of a party,
arranged for beforehand, you are always sure of comfortable quarters. At meal-stations, in out-of-the-way
places, especially through the newer settlements, you
are invariably better cared for than the ordinary traveller; for the keeper of a restaurant, certain of a positive large number, makes generous preparation, where,
for the insecure patronage of usual trains, he could not
run the risk. You travel almost entirely by special
train, which gives more time for refreshment, and does
away with many petty trials, both of delay and hurry.
A lady is enabled to visit places usually out of a
woman's reach, and with no need of personal escort,
since the management takes unusual care of all those
who have no especial protector. Taken as a whole,
your travelling companions are of a far more select
class than would fall to your lot in every-day journeying. To prove this, you have only to walk through the
cars of any regular train, which may from time to time
come in connection with your own. Little courtesies,
in the shape of special time-tables, cards or pamphlets
of information regarding new routes, the personal at-
tendance from point to point of superintendents of
new roads, and scores of other helpful and reassuring
attentions, keep one at ease through the long journey.
And you are *not* obliged to be on terms of absolute
intimacy with every one whose name you find on
your pretty souvenir programme. People will choose
their own particular friends, and will take you or leave
you, just as they see fit, and you will exercise a similar

right. There will be the pleasant, good feeling of a community assimilated by the same desires and same ends, but that is all. You know in the outset the exact amount of expense to be incurred, and can leave what margin for other spending you choose; and, unless you are one of the few dowered with plenty of money, and the still fewer rich in plenty of time, with a good head for planning, and a magnificent genius in the way of executive ability, there is no way on earth by which you can make a pleasure trip so happily.

You will find always, without any doubt, a few professional grumblers, "people who would find fault with heaven because their halo did not fit," as our picturesque young man once put it, who will try to torture you, while they make themselves happy by growling out odious comparisons and sowing spiteful innuendoes. They will try to make you believe that the excursionists are sent to third-class hotels for third-rate accommodations; that they are snubbed by porters and sneered at by waiters; that they travel under a cloud, and, as it were, on sufferance. But use your own eyes and ears; exercise your own intelligence, and prove whether this is so. It is an unfortunate fact in natural history that the manners of the animal man become still more animal in certain situations, and that Western hotel and car service form part of these. But you suffer no more than your neighbor, the regular traveller. There was a Pullman porter on the return trip who used to fling inoffending pillows about with a fine scorn, intended to show that he was meant for better things than making up berths

15

in sleeping-cars, but his reign of terror poured alike
over the just and the unjust. For the rest, here in an
excursion, as well as in every other situation of life,
you will find yourself treated very much as you
deserve. If you are selfish, imperious and domineer-
ing, rude to your fellow-servant, and inflated with the
importance of the sordid, little-souled Ego, who can
stoop to be ungenerous or impolite to an inferior,
then you will be thoroughly hated and genuinely
snubbed, and take my compliments with it; but if you
keep a civil tongue in your head and a kindly thought
in your heart for those who are ministering to your
pleasure or convenience; if you mingle a little humanity with your every-day manners, and have a remnant,
at least, of that true dignity which is above being
wounded by every pin-prick, you will go on healthily
and happily, and find the world what you make it. A
Raymond excursionist has no coupon which absolves
him from the ordinary courtesies of life.

As concerns the means of travel, they are the best
we are capable of yet, though I am surprised to find
the best so bad. In all the years that have elapsed
since the invention of palace and sleeping-cars, it is
discouraging to think so few improvements have been
made in them. There is the same atrocious ventila-
tion, especially at night, when it is Hobson's choice
whether you will suffocate for want of air, or be
smothered by coal dust. There are the same infernal
curtains, hot, heavy and dusty, sealing the sarcophagus
of a berth hermetically, whereas the lightest and thin-
nest muslin drapery would answer all purposes of

concealment and give one a chance-breath for life besides. Stupidity cannot go further than in the continuance of these dreadful woolen draperies, in place of a light, penetrable screening of wire gauze, or something equally clean and porous. To say they are necessary evils, is absurd on the face of it; if Yankee ingenuity cannot meet the question of draughts by any other means than choking the individual to put him out of danger of catching cold, it is certainly wanting in its old-time gumption. There is the same incomplete toilet arrangement, so wofully inadequate to the number of aspirants for cleanliness; and the same unkind distinction between masculine and feminine races, by which the men have twice as much accommodation as the women. This, I am told, is because twice or three times the number of men travel as of women; but, in that case, could not some divison be made by which women alone, or with escorts, could have one car on each train, and have in that car at least equal rights with their husbands or brothers? There would always be more trouble in the lady's car; for the very fact of their being less used to journeying makes them less able to be methodical, and more apt, I am sorry to say, to be inconsiderate to each other. I have seen one inoffensive looking little woman stay thirty minutes bathing, and arranging her hair and dress, while eleven others waited their turn, and the breakfast-station was less than an hour off. But such incomprehensible stupidity does not alter the fact that we ought to have at least equal washing facilities. What is a man's toilet while

travelling, whether or no, but a splutter and splash, a
scrub with a towel, and a momentary tussle with a
hair-brush; a tug at a shoulder-brace and a jerk at a
collar, a twitch at a neck-tie and wrestle with a sleeve-
button, a slap at a vest and dash at a coat,—and there
he is, looking as if he stepped out of a band-box.
But a woman! think of the back-hair and front-hair,
the frizzes and bangs, the underskirts and overskirts
and draperies, the mysteries of the nail toilet, the
artful artlessnesses of neck trimmings, the many-
buttoned boots, the crinoline and pull-backs; think of
the slow and laborious progress toward final perfection, of her dainty deftness and exquisite nicety, and
think of it all in a closet three feet square in a train
going thirty miles an hour, with a dozen anxious and
aimless ones waiting outside and making audible
comments on her slowness! O, it is easy to see that
the sleeping-car is a masculine invention! In order
of excellence, the Pullman comes easily first; it is
roomier, brighter and fresher; its pillows are larger,
and there is some resting-place for the poor, tired
porter. The Silver palace cars come next; they are
nearly as good as the Pullman; the Wagner comes last
of all, and a long way behind. People who do not
travel farther than Chicago have the very poorest appointments; the Wagner has a monopoly of the East.

As the requisites for a California journey, the less
one burdens one's self with the better. There are
certain essentials and a few ameliorations which it
would be well to keep in mind. One wants at almost
any season of the year a strong, plain, comfortable

travelling-dress, short and easy, of some close-grained
woolen material, as absolutely free from trimming as
is consistent with good taste. Trimmings mean dust,
and dust soon means dirt and frowsiness. Gray, with
some decided bit of color about the collar and sleeves,
is best, for gray alone is unbecoming to most people;
peacock-blue is both serviceable and pretty; light
browns are admissible, but dark colors, almost without exception, show the wear and tear of travel sooner
than others. If a second travelling-dress could be
taken to provide against emergencies, it would be
always well; better, if it is thinner than the first, so
that oppressively hot weather might find it available.
An ulster is the most convenient outer wrap, for it
protects the dress and leaves the arms free, and a
gossamer waterproof can be kept in one of its pockets.
The underclothes should be all of gray, light both in
shade and texture; nothing is so wearing as a heavy
weight of clothing borne on hips and shoulders, in
addition to other fatigue. This much of change, with
a pair of easy boots, or slippers for the cars, should
be kept among the hand-luggage in a stout strap. The
toilet arrangements, with a light woolen wrapper or
sacque, for night wear, can go in a satchel. The
trunk can be packed to suit one's self, always remembering that there is no need of an overplus of
changes, as soiled clothes can be laundried at every
city where there is a two-days' rest; and one best
dress, or two at most, makes ample allowance for a
three-months' stay. One wants a dress-hat and mantle
for state occasions; any kind of simple, becoming

head-gear for travelling ; a long tissue veil of silk and wool, which will probably be worn, to the exclusion of everything else about head and neck, in the cars, as a protection from dust and ashes, through most of the journey; a pair of stout boots for rough or stormy walking, and as many pairs of long-wristed gloves as your purse will allow. There is nothing like a railroad trip for using up gloves. By the way, I must not forget the purse itself, and *you* must not forget to put money in it. There are a thousand and one little calls not down on the bills, and not absolutely necessary, but which are sure to come, nevertheless.

A man's needs I cannot speak about so decidedly; whatever sort of trousers will bear wear and tear and look none the worse for it; whatever kind of coat and vest will remain always respectable in the face of insult and injury; whatever manner of suit, in short, will admit of being grimed by soot and ashes, wet by rain, crumpled by sitting up or lying down, and played the mischief with generally, yet always be neat and tidy; that is the kind of stuff they need, whether they buy it at Oak Hall or Randidge's. But I know they want colored shirts, lightly tinted, either wool or cambric, and some loose sailor ties, and as many boots as their female cousins, and two or three hats to be blown away over the plains or in San Francisco harbor. That is the favorite amusement. The Big Boy says they need also a suit of Pjammas, whatever that dreadful sounding article may be.

They need beside, both men and women, plenty of **good humor** and **a** fair share of health, a quiet conscience and a little leaven of consideration. Having which graces, which God has graciously placed within reach of every human, I can wish them no better gift to set them off, than a Russia-leather bound book of coupons for a Raymond excursion to Colorado and California.

INDEX.

THE

DENVER & RIO GRANDE

RAILWAY,

REACHING THE

LEADING PLEASURE RESORTS and SCENIC ATTRACTIONS

OF

COLORADO,

NEW MEXICO,

and UTAH,

AND CROSSING THE

Main Ranges of the Rocky Mountains Eight Times,

FORMS

THE UNEQUALED TOURIST ROUTE

OF THE WORLD.

Connecting the Trunk Lines at Denver and Pueblo with the Central
Pacific Railroad at Ogden, it offers a new and
most attractive highway for

TRANSCONTINENTAL TRAVEL.

SIXTEEN HUNDRED MILES OF MOUNTAIN RAILWAY,

WELL BUILT, ELEGANTLY EQUIPPED, and CAREFULLY MANAGED.

Note. — This system is traversed extensively by Raymond & Whit-
comb's Colorado and California Excursion Parties.

☞ For information, rates and itineraries, address

D. C. DODGE,   F. C. NIMS,

Gen. Manager,   *Gen. Pass. and Ticket Agent,*

DENVER, COLO.

www.ingramcontent.com/pod-product-compliance
Lightning Source LLC
Chambersburg PA
CBHW022006050726
47499CB00006BB/1869